GAY WAS THE PIT

Biography
LORD BOTHWELL
CHANCELLOR THURLOW

Plays
CAN WE TELL?
CYNARA (with H. M. Harwood)
KING QUEEN KNAVE (with H. M. Harwood)
THE KEY (with J. L. Hardy)
THE DEVIL'S GENERAL (with C. Hassell,
from the German of C. Zuchmayer)
FINISHING SCHOOL (with Margaret Gore-Browne)

Novels
THE CRATER
AN IMPERFECT LOVER

Detection
MURDER OF AN M.P.
DEATH ON DELIVERY

ANNE OLDFIELD

1683 – 1730

Artist unknown

GAY WAS THE PIT

THE LIFE AND TIMES OF
ANNE OLDFIELD, ACTRESS
(1683-1730)

BY

ROBERT GORE-BROWNE

MAX REINHARDT : LONDON

FIRST PUBLISHED 1957

Set in Baskerville and printed by
STAPLES PRINTERS LIMITED
at their Rochester, Kent, establishment

Dedicated to

H. M. HARWOOD

remembering happy collaboration

Contents

Prologue

MARGARET SAUNDERS looked down with red eyelids at the lovely, lifeless face.

She had been an actress herself until asthma forced her off the stage to become a dresser. She remembered some lines from one of the first plays her dead mistress, Anne Oldfield, had acted:

Heavens, hussy! If you should – as I hope you won't – outlive me, take care I ain't buried in flannel. 'Twould never become me.

It would be an expensive business circumventing the law, she sighed. You could be fined for disregarding a statute that ordained woollen shrouds. But Margaret Saunders cared little for the wool trade and much for her mistress. She started to dress her for her last public appearance. She chose a holland shift with a tucker and double ruffles of very fine Brussels lace. On the head she arranged a head-dress, too, of very fine Brussels lace. She drew a pair of new, white kid gloves over the stiff fingers. Then the dead woman, who had cared so much for elegance, was ready to lie upon her velvet-draped bier in the Jerusalem Chamber at Westminster.

The motley procession filing by this pathetic grandeur was moved by varying emotions. Love, respect, pity, a feeling for the macabre, drew many. Sardonic curiosity filled Alexander Pope. The dead actress had played lead in a very bad farce in which he had collaborated. It was hissed. Of course, he blamed her. He went home from her lying in state to work on those famous, heartless lines that presented his idea of the dying woman's last moments:

' Odious! In woollen! 'twould a saint provoke!'
(Were the last words that poor Narcissa spoke;)
' No, let a charming chintz and Brussels lace
Wrap my cold limbs and shade my lifeless face;
One would not, sure, be frightful when one's dead,
And, Betty, give this cheek a little red.'

9

She certainly did not look frightful now. The large, expressive, hazel eyes which she used to half-close as she made a comedy point, were quite closed now and for ever. Death had blurred the lines which forty-seven years of life with its emotions, and thirty years of the stage with its pretences, had traced on her gentle features. It had smoothed away the signs of the last months' sufferings. She looked what the poet Campbell averred her, the most beautiful woman that ever trod the boards: Oldfield, ' the fair, the witty and the gay, the Box's charmer and the Pit's delight '. In her years of supremacy on the stage, engaging, bright-eyed, silver-tongued Anne had created the leading rôles of so many of the plays of Farquhar, Steele, Addison, Cibber and Rowe and had acted more than thirty tragedies and sixty comedies. To the crowd who now came to pay her honour, it seemed intolerable to witness her ultimate curtain-call:

> Here, here the poor remains of Oldfield lay,
> *Gay was the Pit* whenever she was gay,
> Coquettes would blush and jilts would envy bear
> To see themselves so well performed in her,
> And every exit echoes with applause. . . .

This, murmured an old play-goer, was the first bad exit Oldfield ever made. He was wrong. It was her most splendid. Between ten and eleven that night they carried her into Westminster Abbey. Two peers and four fine gentlemen supported the pall. Her son by her first notable lover was chief mourner. The service was read by the senior Prebendary of the Abbey, lit only by the faint lights of her procession. With utmost pomp and solemnity she was buried near the monument of William Congreve, who had preceded by only a few months this most dazzling of all his Millamants. Voltaire commented on the different fate accorded the bones of the first French and the first English actress of his day: Adrienne Lecouvreur, refused Christian burial by the bishops, wrapped like a parcel, pushed into a hackney cab, lighted by the torches of two street porters to a piece of waste land near the Seine; and Anne Oldfield, interred among the kings and heroes of her country with the same honour that had just been paid to great Isaac Newton:

Nul art n'est méprisé, tout succès a sa gloire . . .
Et la charmante Ophils et l'immortel Newton
Ont part au temple de mémoire.

In the democracy of death a little drab had risen from the bar of a pot-house in St James's Market, above the grease paint and bawdy of the stage, through the lecherous fingers of the beaux who crowded green room and wings, to a grave in the national Valhalla.

CHAPTER I

What can ennoble sots or slaves or cowards?
Alas! not all the blood of all the Howards.

POPE

Family Tree

THE VULTURES of Grub Street began to gather before Anne's body was carried out of the Jerusalem Chamber.

The first sign of their interest was an advertisement in the *Daily Post* three days after her death:

> To prevent all surreptitious accounts, this is to give notice that I have been some years collecting and compiling *Faithful Memoirs* of the life of Mrs. Anne Oldfield and shall publish the same with all convenient speed in justice to her charming memory. If any person will favour me with authentic notices, the same will be gratefully acknowledged if directed to Hurt's coffee house for W. T. Egerton.

Who was this William Egerton? Was he one of the hack writers of Edmund Curll, bookseller, or was he, perhaps, that insidious tradesman himself? Whoever he might be, he did not long keep the field to himself.

Next day, the day of Anne's Abbey burial, the publisher of a rival production warned the town from the advertisement columns of the *Daily Journal* that only a very false and surreptitious account might be expected from Mr Egerton. But the veracious author of an intended volume of *Authentic Memoirs* could be relied on to adhere strictly to matters of fact, without interspersing a heap of forgeries and inconsistencies.

Two days later this smart piece of journalism saw the light. On superfine Genoa paper, in quarto form, at the moderate price of one shilling, were published the *Authentic Memoirs* of that celebrated Actress Mrs Ann Oldfield, containing a genuine account of her transactions from her infancy to the time of her decease. To this was added a poem to her memory, most submissively inscribed to Brigadier-General Charles Churchill, (with whom Anne was living up to the day of her death).

The author was anonymous although, by the time a fourth edition was called for, he attained the dignity of ' a certain eminent peer of the realm '. He could not resist a dig at his outpaced rival, William Egerton: a *nom de guerre*, he declared, whose owner was so ignorant of his subject that he had even misspelt his heroine's Christian name, writing it with an ' e ', whereas, as was well known, she always signed without one. (And here this battle of books may be interrupted to arbitrate. Both pamphleteers are right. Anne, with contemptuous impartiality, used both spellings, signing for instance one contract with John Vanbrugh at the Haymarket as Ann, and another with Owen Swiney three years later as Anne. Familiarly she was known as Nanny. There is no trace in contemporary written sources of the stage tradition of Nance.)

William Egerton did not throw up the sponge. Soon he announced that *Faithful Memoirs* were in the press and would be published, with Mrs Oldfield's portrait finely engraved, in three weeks' time. Her life and amours would be recorded with a copy of her last will and testament, and also the will of Arthur Maynwaring, her one-time lover. A warning was added against the gross impositions of ' a certain pamphleteer ' and the idle papers that he was having hawked about the streets.

This first author, however, had got off to a good start and retorted with a new edition that contained large amendments and additions: a letter signed T.H. relating to an intrigue between Mrs Oldfield and the late D—— of B——, an epitaph and a full account of her amour with one Mr F . . . e, gent., formerly belonging to the receipt of H.M. Customs. Before the actress had been a month beneath the flagstones of the Abbey, so great an interest did the public still feel in her love-life that a fifth and sixth edition of these revelations was called for. When Egerton's slightly more decorous concoction at last came out in the New Year, it was derided by reviewers as ' a thing without head or tail or form or grace. A wild false, glaring, unconnected mass '.

As relief to these pamphlets numerous, less scandalous, poems and epitaphs appeared: a Pastoral Elegy on the Death of Calista, humbly inscribed to the Hon. Colonel Churchill, price sixpence. Anne had played Calista, frail heroine of Rowe's *Fair*

Penitent, at her last benefit. Another poem on the death of the celebrated Mrs Oldfield, dedicated to the Hon. Brigadier Churchill, was signed by S. Littlemore, gent., and showed some genuine feeling, but the satirical Mainwario's (Maynwaring's) Welcome to Ophelia (Oldfield) cannot be found to have survived the centuries.

Indecent though the haste and scabrous the intention of the two books of memoirs, the information they contain about her family and youth, as Anne's mother and aunt were alive when they were written, may well be true. Her paternal grandfather then was a vintner who rented the *George* tavern in Pall Mall, opposite the more famous *Cocoa Tree.* Inns, then as now, were frequented by all classes. They were free and easy places, and mention is made of a gentleman seen washing his teeth at the window of one in Pall Mall; it may well have been the *George.*

The old man did so well that he ended by buying the house he had rented and the two properties next door, both of which he rebuilt. He had two sons. The elder and steadier, George, was set up as a hosier in fashionable St James's Street. The younger, Anne's father, inherited the inn and the two adjacent houses, worth sixty or seventy pounds a year, enough in those days to manage on. But by the free way he lived, he spent ' this very pretty inheritance ' and ran into debt as well. He first mortgaged his property, then sold it outright to the exemplary George. When he had paid what he owed, with what was left he bought into the Horse Guards. As it was called in his day, he ' rode in the Guards '. There he found men of all ranks of society, mounted on black horses, white feathers in their hats, wearing richly laced coats of scarlet. He was a few years senior to Richard Steele, playwright and essayist, who also in his youth ' rode a private man in the Horse Guards '. Oldfield is said to have risen to hold King James's commission, but who knows if the story of his promotion was not engendered by his daughter's ultimate eminence?

For before an early death he found time to marry and beget a daughter. Anne's mother was better connected, it was claimed, than the inn-keeper's son. Someone has resurrected a marriage between James Oldfield and Elizabeth Blanchard, both of the parish of St Martin-in-the-Fields, at that church, on 4 December

1682. Both parish and date are likely enough, for little Anne was born in Pall Mall during 1683. Unfortunately, from the future actress's will, it appears that her mother's name was Anne. So Elizabeth Blanchard has to give place. There was a marriage between Nathaneel Oldfeild (the spelling is the officiating clergyman's) and Anne Higgins on 26 March 1682 at St James's, Duke Place. This city church does not seem very probable, until it is remembered that its rector was a broad-minded man who made a practice of performing the ceremony without insistence on formalities of licence or banns. Their absence may have suited Trooper Oldfield's casual, or impetuous, turn of mind.

Oldfield was not the sort of man to make old bones and soon his widow was mourning him in discreet poverty. Good Uncle George again stepped in and gave little Anne such education as she was to have. Her extant handwriting does not suggest that it was very elaborate; practical considerations naturally prevailed. A certain Edward Kidder kept a pastry school in Norris Street, St James's Market. There, on Thursday, Friday and Saturday mornings he taught young ladies all sorts of cookery, including ' Dutch hollow works and batter works '. Anne's aunt, Mrs Voss, kept the *Mitre* in St James's Market, so her niece may well have been one of Kidder's pupils. But however illiberal her education, or perhaps because of its deficiencies, Anne acquired a respect for learning. After she had made her mark, she never sent away any person in distress who happened to have had his dose of Latin and Greek.

The days of her schooling were brief. Before long she was put to work for Mrs Wootton, a sempstress who lived in King Street. But as she sewed, she used to read; for so far, at any rate, her education had carried her. Always she read plays and she amused herself by memorizing the parts.

The whole of her young life cannot have been spent sewing and reading. She would obviously find time for less placid pleasures like the dances that girls of her age and class enjoyed: Moll Peatly, Hunt the Spaniard, or Lord Mayor's Delight, but not, of course, ' a most impudent and lascivious step called Setting, the very reverse of back to back '.

At fifteen, she had left Mrs Wootton and was serving in

Aunt Voss's bar at the *Mitre*. Her mother is stated to have married again, this time a Mr Wood, but as she was still to figure as Oldfield in her daughter's will, probably the union was unhallowed in any church. It did not bring much improvement in her worldly condition. She became a mantua-maker. When her daughter was established at Drury Lane, the mantua-maker found work designing gowns for the actresses. Presently young Anne could afford to give her an allowance. As Mrs Saunders the dresser said, Anne was the best of friends and of daughters. Her bounty enabled her mother to retire and ' live very private ' with her sister.

B

CHAPTER II

.... One of those little prating girls
Of whom fond parents tell such tedious tales.

DRYDEN

Beginnings

IT WAS THE last year of the century and one evening a tall
figure with a vaguely military bearing might have been seen
picking its way across the cobblestones of St James's Market.
Familiar with every tavern in London, the wayfarer swaggered
without hesitation through the doorway of the *Mitre*. Tossing a
triangular hat on the bench, he called loudly for wine. A faint
brogue suggested the sister isle. A long, oval face with a high
forehead, full lips and deep lines from nostril to corner of mouth
hinted a sensibility that contradicted the swagger. ' Captain '
George Farquhar was twenty-one, he had just had his first play
produced and the world, he hoped, lay at his feet. But though
Love and a Bottle had run nine nights in its first season, which
was counted a success in those unexacting days, his pockets still
were empty. It took a careful search to settle the score for the
bottle Mrs Voss had brought him.

As he sat drinking, he became conscious of a girl's voice in a
room behind the bar. She was reading aloud. He listened idly.
Something in the words was familiar. Surely he was listening to
a play, and a play he had acted when he was on the Dublin
stage? Beaumont and Fletcher, was it? *The Scornful Lady*? He
had played Young Loveless: one of his better performances, he
flattered himself. He moved to a table nearer the bar. Whoever
the reader, she was doing well. Many years later he told the
prompter at the Theatre Royal: ' With such a just vivacity and
humour of the characters that it gave me infinite surprise and
satisfaction.' His curiosity was aroused and he made some
excuse to Mrs Voss to penetrate to the back quarters of the inn.
Entering the room on tip-toe he was struck dumb at the sight
of the reading girl's blazing beauty and graceful figure. She
looked up and threw down the book in pretty confusion.

George Farquhar's Irish tongue was apt with compliment and ribald banter. But in the barmaid's repartee he found his match. He was astounded, he reported, at her discourse and sprightly wit. He begged her go on with the play, but she refused. Mrs Voss joined them and was less pleased than her niece with the Captain's protestations that the charming reader should forsake the bar and find her vocation on the stage. As soon as she could, the aunt got rid of a Farquhar inwardly resolved to pursue the acquaintance.

Versions of the story now differ, and it may have been he, or it may have been Anne's mother (once servant to Christopher Rich, Patentee of the Theatre Royal) who got in touch with John Vanbrugh, the most popular dramatist then writing. Vanbrugh was persuaded to make a trip to the *Mitre* to judge for himself. Graciously the great man asked Anne which she preferred to read, tragedy or comedy. Tactfully, for she knew Vanbrugh's own line of country, she voted for Thalia and added that she had worked her way through the whole of Beaumont and Fletcher. She artfully professed a distaste for life on the stage, though all the while, as she afterwards told the Drury Lane prompter: ' I longed to be at it and only wanted a little decent entreaty.'

Her feigned reluctance provided the necessary spur and Vanbrugh lost no time in seeing Christopher Rich, Patentee of the Theatre Royal. Anne had shown precocious sign of the intelligent tact that was to distinguish her whole career.

Rich was an old snarling lawyer, who understood poetry, said one of his hack writers, no more than algebra. He gave his actors more liberty and fewer days' pay than any of his competitors. He would laugh with them over a bottle and ' bite ' them over their contracts. He kept them poor so that they might not rebel, and merry that they might not think. Rich had no artistic conscience: Shakespeare or performing seals were equally acceptable. This model impresario, it will be readily understood, made a large fortune and ended up owning race-horses.

Rich had an eye for a pretty girl and when Vanbrugh brought Anne to see him, he promptly engaged her at a salary of fifteen shillings a week. No account of the interview has

survived, but one of Steele's unfinished plays shows what customarily happened when Mama took Daughter for a first
audition:

' To be a maid of honour, a waiting lady on your Statiras and
Roxanas, or any of your theatrical princesses, she'll deserve twenty
shillings a week for mere dumb show ' [begins the manager who has
slightly more lavish ideas than Rich]. ' Let her be for dumb show
only ' [cuts in his partner]. ' Her face is not all. She must be well-
limbed. She may sometimes be in a boy's dress, a cupid, a young
heir to a great family, a page or a gentleman usher.'
    The mother had come prepared.
    ' I have had a model taken of her legs, which you shall see, gentlemen. There they are! As fine a straight leg and as proper a calf! You
shall seldom see a woman's leg so well made.'
    The management is duly impressed:
    ' If the lady pleases to show her face,' [for Mama, with her fine
sense of dramatic effect, had insisted that Daughter should wear a
mask] ' we shall give twenty shillings a week certain.'
    The girl obliges and elicits the ambiguous compliment:
    ' On my word, a very surprising face. May I beg the favour to see
those pretty lips move? ' ' Gentlemen,' [cuts in the mother], ' I beg
she may be kept wholly for tragedy, for she takes prodigiously after
me. She can act only in a haughty part; I was prodigiously haughty
in my youth.'
    'Well, madam, pluck up a spirit,' [the manager encourages the
girl]. ' Let us hear you grace it and do it with an air. Speak it
politely with a side face. You are to imagine an audience though
there is none. . . .'

All goes well. The girl is admitted to the profession and starts
at the bottom of the ladder. One of the early glimpses vouchsafed us of the stately Mrs Siddons is of a shy figure standing in
the wings, knocking a pair of snuffers against a candlestick to
simulate the sound of a windmill in motion.

CHAPTER III

I have no time to read play bills. One merely comes to meet one's friends and show that one's alive.

FANNY BURNEY

Theatre Royal

TO THE HAZARDS of the Theatre Royal, Drury Lane, in the year 1699 at the courageous age of sixteen, came Anne Oldfield to earn her salary of fifteen shillings a week. In fairness to the management it may be mentioned that the only other theatre then licensed, the New Theatre in Lincoln's Inn Fields, paid Betterton, head of the profession, only four pounds a week.

The Theatre Royal was the second on the site. Some fifteen years earlier, it had been built by Sir Christopher Wren on the burned-out ruins of the first, at a cost of four thousand two hundred pounds. Once the theatre-goer had passed a barrage of ladies of the easiest of virtue who infested the pavement, he found himself in a house that would not be unrecognizable by a patron of to-day. The auditorium consisted of an amphitheatre which surrounded a Pit lined with backless benches covered in green cloth. Men of quality patronized the Pit, particularly the younger men, with whom ' some ladies of reputation and virtue, and abundance of damsels that hunt for prey, sit all together, higgledy-piggledy, chatter, toy, play, hear, hear not '. Opposite the stage at the back of the Pit came the Boxes, ' taken by persons of the best quality among whom are generally very few men '. Above the Boxes ran two Galleries where sat the less exalted. To the Upper Gallery, footmen of Box-holders were admitted free for the last act, and formed a noisy, distracting audience. Prices were always going up. To defray the cost of the introduction of scenery D'Avenant, an early Patentee, raised the Pit from one and sixpence to half a crown, seats in the Boxes from half a crown to four shillings, Gallery one shilling to one and sixpence, Upper Gallery sixpence to a shilling. To meet the cost of more elaborate sets for one of Anne Oldfield's great successes, Steele's *Conscious Lovers*, the management doubled the price of the Pit: ' Now what shall we say of these most sordid wretches, whose avarice is no more to be satisfied than the barren womb or the grave? ', asked an embittered habitué.

Turning to the stage itself, the projecting oval, designed by Wren, had recently been truncated by four feet in Rich's determination to squeeze as many rows of seats into the Pit as it could be made to carry. Its shape now was much that of the modern stage. There were side wings and built-in proscenium doorways, through which actors could make their entrances and exits. All action took place in front of the proscenium arch. There were no footlights or, of course, spotlights. Illumination was by large hoops of candles suspended on either side of the stage, which required the constant attention of snuffers. The curtain was not in general use except at the beginning of a play, but the scenery would often open at the back of the set to disclose an additional interior representing a cave, tomb, boudoir or cell. New sets were rare and the same scenery was made to serve in many a successive play.

Perhaps the greatest difference from the theatre of to-day lay in the habits and manners of the audience. In this day of grace the actor has at most to compete with the blasé indifference of the habitual first-nighter; with the discreet fidgets and subdued coughs of a bored dress circle; with late arrival, munching of chocolates and rustling of wrapping paper, by the new plutocracy in the stalls; with eager and untimely passage of teatrays. When an unappreciative infant raises its voice, the interruption evokes a rebuke from a leading actor and a headline in the Press. If the gallery, tried beyond endurance, vents its feelings in half a dozen mild boos, it is presently refused admittance by outraged management. The audience Anne Oldfield had to face was more robust. In the first place it infested the wings and the stage itself. During a performance of *Macbeth*, a certain Earl, who was said ' with some degree of certainty ' to have been in a state of drunkenness for about six years and who had the habit of drinking whiskey during his morning toilet, was haunting the wings. Catching sight of a friend on the prompt side, he crossed the stage through the performers to greet him. The house protested. So did the manager, who threatened, not unreasonably, to exclude the interrupter from future performances. The Earl slapped his face. The manager retaliated. The nobleman's friends threatened to kill the manager but the actors rallied and drove them through the stage door. They returned by the front door and, entering the Boxes, slashed the hangings and broke the sconces. Meanwhile, it may be supposed, Lady Macbeth went quietly on with her sleep-walking.

Sometimes encounters between spectators on the stage led to actual bloodshed. Instance the celebrated duel fought by fifty-year-old Beau Fielding, equerry to the Queen, on the Drury Lane boards. *Faithful Memoirs* places this affair during Anne's benefit performance of Beaumont and Fletcher's *Scornful Lady*, ' when many persons of distinction were behind the scenes '. The Beau, always ' mighty ambitious of showing his fine make and shape ', had the misfortune to jostle a barrister friend of Mrs Oldfield, a certain Mr Fulwood, a man of quick resentment. The outcome was a wound in the Beau's belly, twelve inches deep. Dean Swift, who also reports the encounter, minimizes the depth and location of the injury, stating that Fielding was ' run into his breast which he opened and showed to the ladies that he might move their love and pity. But ', he adds, ' they all fell a-laughing.' The end of the story was less ludicrous. The pugnacious barrister was persuaded out of respect to Mrs Oldfield to leave the theatre. Inveterate play-goer that he was, he proceeded to the Pit of the Lincoln's Inn Fields playhouse where they were giving *The Libertine*. There he met an old enemy in Captain Cusaick, an Irishman. Determined to make an evening of it, he challenged him and took him outside. In less than half an hour word was brought to the theatre that Fulwood was dead and Cusaick in flight.

That is William Egerton's story – a product, it seems, of imperfect memory. The *Daily Courant* records a duel between Beau Fielding and a Mr Goodyear on the stage of Drury Lane during the first night in December 1702 of Farquhar's *Twin Rivals*, in which the female lead was played by Anne's rival, Mrs Rogers. The *Flying Post* reports the incident too:

On Monday last Colonel Fielding, commonly called Handsome Fielding, was dangerously wounded in a quarrel with one, Mr

Goodyear, a gentleman, at the Theatre Royal, Drury Lane. On
Tuesday night last, one Mr Cusaick, an Irish gentleman, and
Captain Fulwood quarrelled at the New Theatre, Lincoln's Inn
Fields and afterwards fought. Captain Fulwood fell on the spot and
Mr Cusaick was dangerously wounded.

The victim was ' very decently ' buried on Sunday evening at
St Clement Danes in the Strand, whither his corpse was brought
in a hearse from the Haymarket.

Small wonder Queen Anne issued a proclamation which,
after desiring that nothing might be acted contrary to religion
and good manners, decreed that no person of what quality
soever should go behind the scenes or come upon the stage
whether before or during the acting of any play: a decree
repeated in different forms at decent intervals and consistently
ignored.

Nor were the elements content to remain in front of the house
more docile. An insensitive age found its relaxation, apart from
the play, in the ' sporting ' events at Hockley-in-the-Hole. There
a famous bull from Tothill was advertised, with ten dogs to fight
it. Ten let-goes at the bull for a guinea a dog, while the biggest
bear in England fought two dogs; a bull, a bear and a ram were
turned loose in the garden with dogs baiting them. Small
wonder if the same public brought the same technique to Drury
Lane. At a first night a sea captain found himself seated between
' a couple of sparks, both prepared with their offensive instruments, vulgarly called catcalls, which they were often tuning
before the play began '. The sailor remonstrated in civil terms.
One of his neighbours was shamed into putting his whistle in
his pocket. The other paid less heed, until ' the squeak was
stopped by a blow. The child's trumpet was struck through his
cheek and his companion led him out to find a surgeon '.

Addison, a less emphatic play-goer, was also concerned with
this abuse.

The night before I left London, [he remarked] I went to see a
play called *The Humourous Lieutenant*. Upon the rising of the curtain
I was very much surprised with the great concert of catcalls.

He goes on to philosophize urbanely about their executant:

He has his bass and his treble catcall, the former for tragedy and the latter for comedy. He has a particular squeak to denote the violation of each of the unities and has different sounds to show whether he aims at the poet or the player.

Sometimes no mechanical aid was invoked. ' One man hisses ', says Fielding, himself a practising playwright, ' out of resentment to the author; a second out of dislike to the house; a third out of dislike to the actor; a fourth out of dislike to the play; a fifth for the joke's sake; a sixth to keep all the rest in company.' Colley Cibber, who, actor and dramatist, had experienced to the full the high spirits of audiences, remarks: ' they come to a new play like hounds to a carcass and are all in full cry, sometimes for an hour together before the curtain rises '.

To combat the public's exuberance on first nights, some authors took refuge in a claque. Sir Richard Steele was one of them.

You [a critic addresses him] have ordered a thirty-pound dinner to be got ready at the *Rose*, where you and your knights of the round table have eat and drunk yourselves up to success. In short you have almost filled the Pit and Galleries with your creatures, who have been ordered at some certain signals to clap, laugh, huzza, to clatter their canes and their heels.

It was said that at the opening night of Benjamin Martyn's play *Timoleon*, when Anne Oldfield spoke the epilogue, the claque was so busy that candle-snuffers were applauded and scene-shifters got a round as they carried on a sofa.

All interruption did not betoken approval or disapproval. Sometimes it was merely light-headed chatter, like the lady's which filled a pause in the tragedy of *Macbeth*, demanding in a loud voice: ' When will the dear witches enter? '; and not long after calling to a young baronet in a neighbouring Box to know if Macbeth's wife was still alive. Sometimes it had its roots in burgundy. A bully beau comes drunk into the Pit and stands on the benches, swearing, ' Damme Jack, 'tis a confounded play, let's to a whore and spend our time better! ' – a verdict any Sunday newspaper critic would envy. Sometimes, of course, the interruption was not unprovoked. A Cordelia of greater experience than virtue, who reached the exit lines in *King Lear* (as then performed):

> Armed in my virgin innocence I'll fly
> My Royal Father to relieve or die;

was met with a horse laugh, ' which turned to ridicule this scene of generous pity and compassion '.

Another habit that must have maddened the players sprang from a rule of the theatre, which returned the price of his seat to the spectator who left before the end of the first act:

' Oh! what pleasure 'tis,' [says Sir Novelty Fashion], ' at a good play to go out before half an act's done! '
  ' Why at a good play? ' [asks Narcissa innocently].
  ' Oh, Madam! it gives the whole audience the opportunity of turning upon me at once. And then again it shows my contempt of what the dull town think their chiefest diversion. . . .'

Another character describes his evening's entertainment:

' I dine, drink a bottle, go to Wills, go behind the scenes, make love in the Green Room, take a benefit ticket, ferret the Boxes, straddle into the Pit, Green Room again, do the same in both houses and stay in neither. . . .'

One almost wonders what made Voltaire, that amateur of the English stage in the century's opening years, describe the theatre as ' the noblest and most useful thing invented by the human mind to form and polish morals and manners '!

⋆   ⋆   ⋆

So much for audiences. What of the stage itself when Anne made her début? Instead of the careful period productions of to-day, actors played in very much the costumes of their every-day life. Macbeth would stride, no dim figure from a Celtic twilight but wearing the topical regimentals of scarlet coat and gold braid, crowned by a powdered peruke. No meticulous research planned Cato's toga and tonsure, but a flowing wig and a flowered gown offered acceptable familiarity to the new Augustans. True, a few conventions were preserved:

> To some, prescriptive right gives settled things,
> Black wigs to murderers, feathered hats to kings.

Personal taste was paramount. Robert Wilks, that promising

newcomer from Ireland, liked to wear a red velvet suit with gold Brandenburgs, whatever his part.

But, at the date of Anne's first appearance, Robert Wilks was still small fry. Head and shoulders above the rest of the profession stood the three B's, as they were dubbed with a grain of malice: Betterton, Barry and Bracegirdle. At this period it was to the theatre in Lincoln's Inn Fields that play-goers flocked to applaud them. They were the old guard and their style of acting was of the old school.

Thomas Betterton's ' grave action ' was judged to be without equal. It preserved the medium, said a brother actor, between mouthing and meaning too little, though our generation, nursed on the casual diction of R.A.D.A., would doubtless dub it ' pure ham '. Passionate feeling, variety in characterization, judicious use of voice, avoidance of long pauses calculated to win cheap applause, were excellencies which his contemporaries remarked. When he played Hamlet and the Ghost appeared, his naturally ruddy face, they said, went as pale as his neckcloth. That this need be no exaggeration, those who have watched the back of Alfred Lunt's neck grow pink with embarrassment can testify.

Betterton had fat, short arms which he rarely lifted higher than his stomach; his left hand lodged between coat and waistcoat; his right hand punctuated his speech. The placing of the hands was traditional: the left pressed against the heart, while the elegant motions of the right indicated what that heart was feeling. Betterton's gestures were few but just. His voice was low and grumbling, but he could tune it to an artful climax that caught the attention even of beaux and orange girl. He went on acting until he was an old man. At sixty-seven he was still playing the young Bassanio.

Mrs Barry was a fine creature but not handsome. Her mouth twisted to the right. She had darkish hair, dark eyebrows and bright eyes. Middle-sized, she was inclined to be plump. Actresses of her time relied more on facial expression than the remoteness of present-day audiences allows. They approached the technique of our cinema. Mrs Barry's face, it was remarked, ' ever expressed the passions '. This expression preceded, it was said, her gesture and her gesture preceded the line. Her voice was full, clear and strong, equal to any demands the violent emotions of the part put upon it. But in tender passages, she had an unexampled power of exciting pity. The only reproach that could be levelled at her was a certain lack of tone in her diction, a fault she shared with her contemporaries. In comedy she had less distinction; she neither danced nor sang.

Her reputation was not faultless. One disillusioned admirer stated that if you were with her all night, she would not know you next morning, unless you had another five pounds to put at her disposal!

Mrs Bracegirdle, on the other hand, was credited with a natural frigidity, largely, it seems, because she resisted Congreve's and Rowe's importunities. She was the darling of the public, and such is the illusion of the stage that few spectators, says a down-to-earth observer, who were not past it could behold her without desire. She had dark brown hair and eyebrows, black sparkling eyes, a fine set of white teeth and a ' blushy ' complexion. Although she had no greater claim to strict beauty than ' any other desirable brunette ', her liveliness and glowing health cast their spell. She was of a ' lovely ' height and possessed a good figure, with handsome legs and feet. In breeches parts, where she was particularly admired, her walk was declared free, modest and manlike. Comedy was her *forte* and she had a nice singing voice.

As the three B's were acting at the rival theatre, they had less influence on the formation of Anne's style than Susanna Verbruggen, star of Drury Lane. In her youth, she too had been addicted to breeches parts but, by the time Anne joined the company, she was unkindly described as having thick legs and thighs and a corpulent, large posterior. Her face had preserved its fine, smooth oval and, what was then considered attractive, was marked with ' beautiful and well-disposed moles, as were her neck and breast '. She had not outlived her art, an art ' dressed so nice that it looked like nature. Whatever she did was not to be called acting, no, no, she was the character she represented '. Two opposed rôles were her favourites: the fine, laughing lady, flirting her fan with an affected twitter, and the oafish country girl, with broad, laughing voice, poking head, round shoulders and ' unconceiving ' eye. Susanna was a natural comedienne and never essayed tragic parts. Her realistic style left its mark on her disciple.

In the eighteenth century, stock plays and parts were the theatre's lifeblood and what was called ' possession of parts ' was the undisputed rule. To possess a part might depend on talent, but more often on seniority. A part belonged to an actor as surely as his salary. As there were comparatively few actors to be watched, an audience of regular theatre-goers knew each one's mannerisms in the parts he possessed. For the present, even had she the skill, no stock leading part could be offered to the girl whom Farquhar and Vanbrugh had picked for future greatness.

CHAPTER IV

There is a mode in plays as well as clothes.

DRYDEN

Début

AFTER, FOR NEARLY a year, she had played ladies-in-waiting, pages, and young heirs, ' almost a mute, and unheeded ', opportunity of a sort knocked at Anne's door. A certain Mrs Cross, who was esteemed more for her dancing (and no doubt other qualities) than for her acting, ' made an excursion to France with a certain baronet '. Unexpectedly, an understudy had to be found to play her unimportant part of Candiope, a pathetic princess, in Dryden's tragi-comedy *Secret Love*, which was being rehearsed for Mrs Kent's benefit. Anne was given the chance. No record of her performance has been, or is likely to be, traced. It must have been satisfactory enough; soon Vanbrugh was backing his fancy to cast her for lead in a revival of Fletcher's *Pilgrim* which he was refurbishing, turning its blank verse into prose to suit the taste of the day. Before, however, this production reached the stage, Anne had appeared in February 1700 in the small part of Sylvia, ' a Roman Lady ', in an opera by John Oldmixon set to Purcell's music. Farquhar wrote the epilogue and the deduction is that Anne owed her part to his influence.

The Pilgrim was a more important production. It was the first play to be acted at Drury Lane in the new century, which was considered, on the calendar then in use, to begin on 25 March 1700, the first night of this revival. Not only had John Vanbrugh altered and added to the piece, but the great Dryden's dying hand had written a new prologue, epilogue and secular masque. He had also contributed dialogue between two mad lovers shut up in a lunatic asylum into which the play writhed its picaresque way. The poet laureate was to have the customary author's benefit of the third night's takings, but according to the unreliable Egerton he died that night and the much needed benefit went to his son. As Dryden died on 1 May, Egerton's story may

30

be dismissed with little but admiration for his dramatic instinct. Vanbrugh cast *The Pilgrim* himself. He read it to Colley Cibber, a young actor whose comic talent he admired. Cibber could find nothing in it for himself except two small character parts, the Stuttering Cook and the Mad Englishman. Vanbrugh therefore was free to cast two up-and-coming actors for his male leads: hard-working Robert Wilks as Pedro the pilgrim, and brilliant, dissolute George Powell as Roderigo the bandit. For his leading lady he took a chance on the novice Oldfield. To Cibber, to make up for his insignificant share, he allocated Dryden's epilogue. That delighted the actor for it was written, he felt, ' much above the strain of common authors '. He rehearsed the lines, which gave an explanation of the immorality of the Court-favoured stage:

> Whitehall the naked Venus first revealed
> Where standing, as at Cyprus, in her shrine
> The strumpet was adored with rites divine . . .

Dryden was so pleased with Cibber's rendering that he paid him the compliment of entrusting the prologue, too, to his tongue. This distinction upset the rest of the company. Wilks was especially irritated. He had a quick temper and never minced his words. It was an insult to the whole company, he shouted, to suppose only one actor capable of speaking prologue and epilogue. Wilks, noted Cibber comfortably, had many excellencies, and if prologue-speaking were left out, he still would have been a valuable actor.

As for the play itself, a modern audience would judge it a queer jumble. Alfonso, strict parent, is determined that his daughter Alinda (Anne) shall marry the man of his choice, who happens, curiously enough, to be an outlaw (Powell). Anne, given to indiscriminate charity to beggars and pilgrims, has fallen in love with one of them, played by Wilks. She escapes her father's custody to follow the handsome vagabond. Clad in the inevitable boy's disguise, she joins Powell's band of outlaws, of course escaping recognition. Wilks falls into their power and Anne is ordered by the implacable Powell to hang him with her own hands. She successfully begs his life and then makes good her escape. The rest of the play tells the tale of her wanderings.

The whole cast fetch up in a lunatic asylum where Anne, affecting to be one of its inmates, takes her father on a conducted tour in the robust eighteenth-century conviction that there is something very funny about the mentally afflicted. At the end of the inspection the father is himself shut up, like Malvolio. In further adventures the versatile Anne, for no very obvious reason, disguises herself as a witch and later as a shepherdess. In the final scene the bandit is restored to respectable society, resigning Anne's hand to her pilgrim lover. To this satisfactory arrangement the father gives a deferred blessing and calls for Dryden's secular masque in honour of the new century.

This farrago had a moderate success and Anne was given a benefit night in July, late in the season, when audiences were scanty. According to the Drury Lane prompter, she had charmed a play which Vanbrugh had revived especially for her, into a run of many succeeding nights. Chetwood was always one of her fans but Cibber from the wings formed a less favourable impression.

Mrs Oldfield [he says severely] had been a year in the Theatre Royal before she was observed to give any tolerable hope of her being an actress, so unlike to all manner of propriety was her manner of speaking.

Of her playing he remarks more kindly that the want of confidence, which is natural to beginners, seemed appropriate to the gentle character of Alinda. Without some such diffidence the tyro never, in Cibber's opinion, goes far.

Nevertheless [he continues], I own I was then so far deceived in my opinion of her, that I thought she had little more than her person that appeared necessary to the forming of a good actress. For she set out with so extraordinary diffidence that it kept her too despondingly down to a formal, plain, (not to say) flat manner of speaking. Nor could the silver tone of her voice, till after some time, incline my ear to any hope in her favour.

It is easy to imagine the paralysing stage-fright which beset the little seventeen-year-old, lifted from behind the bar of the *Mitre* by the favour of the great Vanbrugh, and terrifyingly cast by him in the lead of this important revival. Her whole future and the future of her mother and family hung on her success. Conscious of the imperfection of her vowels, she had to damp

down her silver voice and, in the effort to achieve correctness
of accent, produced the stereotyped, flat diction which Cibber
so emphatically deplored. Almost totally without experience
(Candiope and Sylvia were slight training for carrying a difficult
play on her narrow shoulders) she had no technique to fall
back on or anything to help her but her youth, beauty and the
natural sense of the stage which had set her reading Beaumont
and Fletcher to ' Captain ' Farquhar. But, and even Cibber
admits this, she pleased the public. ' Public Approbation ', he
philosophizes, ' is the warm Weather of a Theatrical Plant,
which will soon bring it forward to whatever Perfection Nature
has designed it.' The rowdy, sensual audiences eyed Alinda's
long, slender legs in their revealing boy's travesty and mentally
pinched her firm buttocks. They were titillated by her demure
beauty and feasted on her youth. In Chetwood's words, she
charmed the play into a run. It entered the Drury Lane
repertory of successful plays and with songs added was later
converted into what was called an opera.

Anne was soon to find that one swallow did not make a
summer. Her *genre* was the same as Mrs Verbruggen's, who was
in possession of all the parts the newcomer would have liked
to play. ' For want of fresh parts ', says the invaluable Cibber,
' Mrs Oldfield seemed to come but slowly forward.'

True, that coming playwright Mrs Centlivre, at her very
good friend Farquhar's request, gave her the ' meaty ' part of
Aurelia in her new play, produced in the summer of 1700. It
was a tragedy called *The Perjur'd Husband*. Anne, in love with
that forsworn character, is killed in a duel by the outraged
wife. She also spoke the prologue. The play was a ' flop ' and
when it appeared in print, Susan Centlivre, with a certain
feminine lack of sportsmanship, laid its failure to the count of the
actors. They were the best, she said slightingly, available at that
late season of the year when the stars had gone to the country.
Besides Anne Oldfield, Mrs Centlivre had the eminently safe
actor Mills as the perjured husband and the inimitable cuckold
Dicky Norris as the noble Venetian, who is fooled by his
wife's maid in the best scene of the play. But then, Susannah
Centlivre will be discovered to have had personal reasons for
blaming a young and beautiful rival for her ill-success.

c

CHAPTER V

A very merry, dancing, drinking,
Laughing, quaffing and unthinking time.

DRYDEN

First Love

ANNE'S FRIENDSHIP with George Farquhar, begun in the parlour behind the bar of the *Mitre*, had ripened. In after years, with a twinkle in her expressive eyes, she would refer primly to agreeable hours she had spent in Mr Farquhar's company. Grub Street was more outspoken. Her uncle, who owned the inn, made her his ' bar-keeper '; and ' she soon enamoured the heart of a gentleman who frequented the house and soon after she left her uncle and went and lived with the said gentleman '.

George Farquhar was bred in Ireland to the Church like his father before him. His residence at Trinity College, Dublin, was cut short after an unseemly comparison with the immunity from drowning of those born to be hanged and Christ's walking on the water. Professionless, he drifted to the Smock Alley Theatre, where he was said to have played Othello as his first part – surely a bold début. He was not a success as an actor and an accident with the foils in a Dryden play, which nearly proved fatal to his opponent, decided him to resign. A loan of ten guineas from Robert Wilks enabled him to try his luck in London. This was a couple of years before he met Anne. In the interval he acquired some sort of a commission in the Army, though his claim to the rank of Captain was nebulous. ' I am called Captain ', he was to write of a character in one of his plays, ' by all the coffeemen, drawers, whores and groom-porters in London. For I wear a red coat, a sword, a hat *bien troussé*, a martial twist in my cravat, a fierce knot in my periwig, a cane upon my button and dice in my pocket.'

For a living he depended on his pen. His first, very bawdy, comedy *Love and a Bottle* was followed by an autobiographical novel. Then a second play at Drury Lane scored a wild success. This was *The Constant Couple or a Trip to the Jubilee* (for 1700 was Jubilee Year at Rome, ' when Popish zealots of all countries

34

make their trip there to buy pardons and trinkets for the convenience of their souls and bodies '). The *ingénue* part of Angelica was one which Anne would have been glad to play. This intolerably modest character is taken by the hero Sir Harry Wildair for an inmate of a brothel, for he has been tricked into believing her ultra-respectable mother to be the madam. Not Anne, but the far more experienced young actress Jane Rogers was cast for the part, and the seeds of a jealousy were sown that was to endure for Jane's life. To be fair, Farquhar had little say in the casting and Jane was five years Anne's senior in the company. Moreover she specialized in the implacably moral type. She would even welcome indifferent parts provided ' they stood in the favourable light of honour and virtue '. Perhaps an episode at the beginning of her stage career influenced her. On the first night of Vanbrugh's *Relapse* (appropriately sub-titled *Virtue in Danger*) George Powell was so drunk and ardent that Cibber, playing Lord Foppington, thought ' it was all up with Mrs Rogers ', who had to play opposite the inebriated hero. At all events she developed a theatrical prudery, which very nearly, said the gossips, succeeded in keeping her chaste; ' study to live the character I play ' was her motto, taken from an epilogue had she once had to speak in a play called *The Triumph of Virtue*.

Jane was not beautiful, but she was tall, had a good figure and nice manners (' exceedingly genteel ' was the contemporary phrase). Living up to her motto, she resisted the temptations offered by ' the most accomplished young noblemen', which mainly embraced the offer of lavish settlements. But Jane was not mercenary. For her first five years of Drury Lane her professional admiration of virtue was reflected in her private life. Then a brother actor laid siege. Robert Wilks, playing Wildair to her Angelica, threatened off-stage to kill himself for love. To save his life, as she was often to remind him, she yielded. Soon she was pregnant. Alas! as Wilks' biographer was to moralize, she quickly found that animal pleasures are never lasting. A Mrs Anne Brett, a society woman, could bring up bigger guns. ' She not only honoured Wilks with her love but with very valuable presents.' The return she exacted was the abandonment of the actress and the daughter she bore. But

though real life romance had faded, Rogers and Wilks were
condemned to act passionate love on the stage, quarrelling
bitterly as they professed it. One night the brutal audience of
the day got its money's worth. Playing the love scenes in *Venice
Preserv'd*, Mrs Rogers' antipathy ' rose to so astounding a pitch
that, the part obliging Mr Wilks to embrace the lady very
close, she laid hold of the opportunity and gave his cheek so
handsome a bite that the mark of her teeth remained and the
blood followed very plentifully '.

⋆   ⋆   ⋆

If Jane Rogers had cause to be professionally jealous of the
much more beautiful, if far less experienced, young actress who
had been pitchforked into her society, another talented girl had
more personal grounds for complaint. This was Susannah
Centlivre, who had to endure Anne's appearance in her play
The Perjur'd Husband.

Susannah's maiden name was Freeman and she spent her
early youth in county circles at Holbeach, Lincolnshire. Left an
orphan at twelve, before reaching years of discretion she started
alone on a journey to London. A Cambridge undergraduate
came to her rescue and soon she was living with him in boy's
clothes at St John's College. The somewhat supine authorities
at length intervened and hurried her off to London, where at the
age of sixteen, beloved of literary ladies, she was married, ' or
something like it ', says her cynical biographer, to a nephew of Sir
Stephen Fox. After a year, she was divorced – or something like
it. Her next matrimonial venture was a Captain Carroll. He was
addicted to duelling, and after a year and a half of marriage
fell victim to his foible. Before she was twenty, Susannah offered
her first play, appropriately entitled *Love at a Venture*, to the Drury
Lane management. They turned it down but the authoress got
it acted at Bath and played in it herself. She was something of
an actress, for five or six years later she went to Windsor to play,
improbably enough, the part of Alexander the Great. There she
met Mr Centlivre, head cook to Queen Anne.

While she was still Susan Carroll, she came into competition
with Anne for the vagrant affections of George Farquhar. The
playwright's polygamous instincts are disclosed in three collections of love letters that he published to relieve his chronic

penury during the early years of the century. There are four major, pseudonymous addressees: Astræa, Penelope, Celia and Chloe. Astræa sometimes comes into the open as Mrs C . . . l, that is Susan Carroll. Penelope was Anne, as an old army officer ' who very well knew Mr Farquhar and some of his youthful gallantries ' told Oldys, author of the 1750 article on the dramatist in *Biographia Britannica*. Farquhar himself admits in his preface to one of the collections that ' a great part of this book was first designed for one of that sex and the beauties of this book, if any there be, were brought from a lady's cabinet '. The identity of the lady is revealed by Farquhar's earliest editor, who says that some of these letters were returned to the playwright by Mrs Oldfield.

No surnames can be supplied for Celia and Chloe, but their circumstances make it plain that these were not poetic synonyms for Susan or Anne. Celia lived in the country, as repeated allusions to brooks, glades, shades and streams indicate. Chloe, though she was not much older than Anne, was not pretty – ' if you expect a beauty ', wrote the Captain ungallantly, ' she won't answer expectation. She's but a girl not eighteen. She sings tolerably and you'll allow her to have some wit.' Moreover, Chloe had a miscarriage and had to leave London at the time Anne was appearing as Alinda in *The Pilgrim*.

To Anne's feelings about her lover, we have only his letters (quoted in the next chapter) as a clue. An actress in embryo would be less than human did she not feel a little flattered by the love-making of a dramatist with Farquhar's record. But there is evidence that she never tried to cash in on his standing. More surely would she ache to mother the improvident, rake-helly young genius, to rescue him from his leaning to the bottle and check the harvest of disease which he was busy sowing. Rare is the woman who is not quite sure she can reform her man, and God knows, George stood in need of reformation. Of course it was a compliment to be picked out by such a connoisseur. But passion the young libertine did not inspire. Such flame as lit the affair burned in Farquhar's easy heart. However unfaithful he was to Anne, he could never quite put her out of his head. This is evident from a passage in *The Constant Couple* which has escaped the lynx eyes of his editors.

Sir Harry Wildair is discussing his latest find with gallant Colonel Standard and that snake in the grass, Mr Vizard. Sir Harry is Farquhar's inevitably autobiographical self:

Wildair	I had an account that she lodged somewhere in St James's.
Standard	Her name pray, Sir Harry? Perhaps we know her?
Wildair	Her name? She has the softest, whitest hand that ever was made of flesh and blood – her lips so balmy sweet!
Standard	But her name, sir?
Wildair	Then her neck and breast! (*sings*) ' Her breasts do so heave, so heave . . .'
Vizard	But her name, her quality?
Wildair	Then her shape, Colonel!
Standard	But her name I want, sir!
Wildair	Then her eyes, Vizard – if you must have it, she is called the Lady ——, but then her foot, gentlemen, she dances to a miracle. . . .

It turns out that this paragon, whose description may as well have been inspired by Anne as by any other of the dramatist's overlapping fancies, is also the admired of Colonel Standard and (secretly) of Mr Vizard. Faced with the prospect of a duel, Sir Harry has second thoughts:

> Fight? Let me consider. I love her, that is true – but then I love honest Sir Harry Wildair better. The lady is divinely charming – but then a thrust i' the guts is as ugly as the devil.

Vizard suggests a counter-attraction:

Vizard	A girl of sixteen, Sir Harry!
	[Anne was sixteen when Farquhar met her.]
Wildair	Now sixteen thousand blessings light on thee!
Vizard	Pretty and witty.
Wildair	Ay, ay, but her name, Vizard?
Vizard	Her name? Yes, she has the softest, whitest hand that was ever made of flesh and blood, her lips so balmy sweet!
Wildair	Well, well, but where shall I find her, man?
Vizard	Find her? But then her foot, Sir Harry! She dances to a miracle.
Wildair	Prithee, don't distract me.
Vizard	Well then, you must know that this lady is the curiosity and ambition of the town. Her name's Angelica. She that passes for her mother is a private bawd . . . I suppose

twenty or thirty pieces handsomely placed will gain the
point. . . .

Standard   With the generality of women, I grant you these arts may
prevail.

Wildair   Generality of women? They're all alike, sir. I never heard
of one that was particular – but one.

Standard   Who was she, pray?

Wildair   *Penelope, I think she's called and that's a poetical story too.*

Why drag in the name Penelope and pay her disinterested
heart a gratuitous compliment, unless the playwright was so
full of his little conquest and her amazing difference from the
rest of her mercenary sex, that he could not keep her off his pen?

It was all the reward she got. While he was writing her
passionate letters, he was writing no less passionately to Celia;
he was getting Chloe with child; he was being challenged to
duels by Astræa's pugnacious husband. No wonder Anne soon
sent him about his business and made it up with Susan. So that,
in spite of that authoress's slighting reference to Anne in the
preface to *The Perjur'd Husband*, she cast her for leading parts in
nine of her fifteen plays. In the preface to the best of them,
The Wonder: A Woman keeps a Secret, she gave proof that the old
rivalry had turned into partnership:

The poet and player [she wrote] are like soul and body indis-
pensably necessary to one another. I freely acknowledge myself
obliged to the actors in general and to Mr Wilks and Mrs Oldfield
in particular and I owe them this justice to say that their inimitable
action could only support a play at such a season and among so many
benefits. I must . . . own that they much outdid in action the
strongest of my conceptions. For though nature was my aim in the
last act, yet nature herself, were she to paint a love quarrel, would
only copy them.

This easy relationship was to develop with the years. When
Anne was starting at Drury Lane, she had nothing but her
beauty and her natural kindness and wit to help her keep her
foothold in the struggling, immoral, jealous, talented universe
she had forced her way into. Farquhar, Wilks, Mrs Rogers,
Mrs Centlivre are only four of the luminaries that studded her
firmament. It was a testing, anxious time. George, her lover,
was little help to her. Anne had to rely on her own character.

CHAPTER VI

Did you ever hear of Captain Wattle?
He was all for love and a little for the bottle.
C. DIBDIN

Love Letters

IT IS TIME to quote from the letters Farquhar had been writing to his young mistress. Except where the name Penelope occurs, a certain amount of detective instinct is needed to pick out the ones designed for Anne's expressive eyes. Astræa, Celia et cetera, divide the rest.

The following pen portrait of the dramatist was addressed to the intelligent, ineligible young actress in the early days of their love affair:

In pursuance to your order, madam, I have sent you here inclosed my picture, and I challenge Vandyck or Kneller to draw more to the life. You are the first person that ever had it and if I had not some thoughts that the substance would fall to your share, I would not part with my likeness.

The dramatist's analysis of his external appearance and of his mental processes, no doubt coloured to impress his feminine reader, follows:

My outside is neither better nor worse than my Creator made it. I have a body qualified to answer all the ends of creation and that's sufficient. As to the mind, 'tis generally dressed like my person in black. Melancholy is its everyday apparel and it has hitherto found few holidays to make it change its clothes. In short my constitution is very splenetic and yet very amorous, both of which I endeavour to hide, lest the former should offend others and the latter might incommode myself. And my reason is so vigilant in restraining these two failings that I am taken for an easy-natured man by my own sex and an ill-natured clown by yours. I am a very great epicure, for which reason I hate all pleasure that is purchased by excess of pain. I am seldom troubled with what the world calls airs and caprices, and I think it an idiot's excuse for a foolish action to say ' 'twas my humour '. I can't relish a jest that vexes another in earnest; in short if I ever do a wilful injury, it must be a very great one. I am often melancholy but seldom angry. I am easily deceived, but then I never fail at last to find out the cheat. I have naturally a propensity to ease that I cannot cheerfully fix to my study, which makes me inclined to poetry above anything else. I have very little estate but what lies under the circumference of my hat. . . .

By now, carried away by his zest for self-revelation, he begins to wonder whether he has not lost sight of his object of exciting his correspondent's sympathy. He applies himself to win it back:

I have something in my outward behaviour which gives strangers a worse opinion of me than I deserve. I have many acquaintances, very few intimates, but no friend. And the greatest proof of my affection that a lady must expect is this: I would run any hazard to make us happy, but would not for any transitory pleasure make either of us miserable.

The next letter is somewhat vaguely dated Friday night, eleven o'clock:

If you find no more rest from your thoughts in bed than I do, I could wish you, madam, to be always there, for there I am most in love. I went to the play this evening and the music raised my soul to such a pitch of passion that I was almost mad with melancholy.

The piece was no doubt the Purcell opera in which Anne took part.

I flew thence to Spring Gardens, where with envious eyes I saw every man pick up his mate, while I alone walked like solitary Adam before the creation of his Eve. Nothing I found entertaining but the nightingale, which methought in sweet notes like your own, pronounced the name of my dear Penelope, ' as the fool thinketh, the bell clinketh '. From thence I retired to the tavern, where methought the shining glass represented your fair person and the sparkling wine within it looked like your lively wit and spirit. I met my dear mistress in everything and I propose presently to see her in a lively dream, since the last thing I do is to kiss her dear letter, clasp her charming Idea in my arms and so fall fast asleep.

The following Night Thought (there is no means of dating the letters) shows that Anne had advanced far enough in her profession to be on very good terms with the star of Drury Lane.

Well! Mrs V[erbruggen] and my charming Penelope are to lie together to-night. What would I give to be a mouse (God bless us!) behind the hangings to hear the chat. You don't know, madam, but my genius, which always attends you, may overhear your discourse – therefore not one word of George!

George goes on to wish lewdly that he was in the place of Mrs Verbruggen or even in the chair occupied by Anne's dog, Monsieur Adonis. Mention of her pet induces verse of a sort:

> My rival is a dog of parts,
> That captivates the ladies' hearts. . . .

which celebrates Adonis's exploit in scaring off a water-rat that frightened Anne, as she walked with Farquhar round Rosamund's Pool in St James's Park. The letter ends; ' now good-morrow, my fair creature, and let me know if you are recovered from your fright.'

Another letter deplores some passing ailment of Anne's. Anxiety became so acute that the playwright went to the length of entertaining ideas of marriage.

Your indisposition last night, when I left you, put me into such disorder that, not finding a coach, I missed my way and never minded whither I wandered till I found myself close to Tyburn. I fell to pitying poor Mr Farquhar who, whilst he roved abroad among your whole sex, was never out of his way and now, by a single she, was led to the gallows. From thoughts of hanging, I naturally entered upon those of matrimony – why should I not hazard the noose to ease me of my torment? Then I considered whether I should send for the ordinary of Newgate or the parson of St Ann's. But considering myself better prepared for dying in a fair lady's arms than on the three-legged tree, I was the most inclinable to the parish priest. Besides, if I died in a fair lady's arms, I should be sure of a Christian burial and should have the most beautiful tomb in the universe. . . .

St Ann's is the parish church of Soho but a play on the name may confirm the identification of Penelope with Anne Oldfield.

These day-to-day jottings bear frequent evidence of poor Farquhar's failing, which he had undertaken to confess:

I can no more let a day pass without seeing or writing to my dear Penelope than I can slip a minute without thinking of her. Let me

therefore confess to my dearest angel how last night I sauntered to
the *Fountain* where some friends waited for me. One of them was a
parson who preaches over anything but his glass. Had not his company and Sunday night sanctified the debauch, I should be very fit
for repentance this morning. The searching wine has sprung the
rheumatism in my right hand, my head aches, my stomach pukes,
I dreamed all this morning of fire, and waked in a flame. To complete my misery, I must let you know all this and make you angry
with me. I design, though, this afternoon to repair to St Ann's
prayers, to beg absolution of my Creator and my mistress. If both
prove merciful, I'll put on the resolution of amending my life to fit
me for the joys of heaven and you.

Apparently he did not find Anne and forgiveness, for the
next scrap seems to run straight on:

Now I write with my aching hand and the distastes of my aching
heart. My body and soul are of a piece, both uneasy for want of my
dear Penelope. Excuse me, madam, for troubling you with my
distemper, but my hand is so ill that it can write nothing else,
because it can go no further.

Several other unquoted letters allude to the rheumatism in
his right hand. The following adventure suggests the start of a
more serious sickness:

Misfortunes always lay hold on me when I forsake my Love or
fall short of my duty. Your coach was full and Mr C[ibbe]r was
vanished, so I had no pretence left to avoid some sober friends that
would haul me into a dark cellar to drink Cider. A dark, chilly,
confounded hole fit only for treason and tobacco. Being warm with
the throng of the playhouse, I unadvisedly threw off my wig. The
rawness of this cursed place, with the coldness of the tipple, has
seized on me so violently that I'm afraid I shalln't recover from it in
a trice. I have got such a pain in my jaws that I shalln't be able to
eat a bit. So now, madam, I must either live upon love or starve. If
you don't send me some comfort in my afflictions, expect to have a
note to this purpose: ' pleased to accompany the corpse of an unfortunate lover who died of an aching chops and a broken heart.'

He was well enough to go to Dryden's funeral. His letter
describing it contains no proof that it was addressed to Anne,
but he could count on the actress's interest in the ceremony,

playing as she then did in a production in which the corpse had
been involved.

I am come now from Mr Dryden's funeral, where we had an ode
of Horace sung instead of David's psalms, whence you may find that
we don't think a poet worth a Christian burial. The pomp of the
ceremony was a kind of rhapsody and fitter I think for Hudibras
than him, because the cavalcade was mostly burlesque. [A rhapsody
was theatre slang of the day for an elaborate stage spectacle.] But
he was an extraordinary man and buried after an extraordinary
fashion . . . and so much for Mr Dryden whose burial was the same
as his life, variety and not of a piece: the quality and the mob, farce
and heroicks, the sublime and ridicule mixed in a piece, great
Cleopatra in a hackney coach.

The spectacle moves Farquhar to draw the moral:

And now, madam, for the application. Let us consider that we are
all mortal, that neither wit can protect a man, nor beauty a woman,
from the impertinence of a burial. There is but one way. Let us join
our forces to disappoint it, as thus: beauty causes love, love inspires
poetry and poetry makes wit immortal. So in return, wit is fired with
gratitude, that extolls your charms and so makes beauty immortal.
Now, madam, if your beauty can make as mad work in my head as
it has in my heart, I will show the world such a copy of your coun-
tenance that you shall be as fair a hundred years hence, as you are
at this instance. All the worms in the churchyard shall not have
power to touch one feature in your face.

That was written in May 1700. By the beginning of August
the dramatist was in Holland. A bad poem of his survives,
explaining that he was detained by a storm:

> Deprived of love and your blest sight I die,
> Whilst you the first and storms the rest deny.

But after who knows what scenes from her and what lies
by him, the love affair had reached its term. It was not
renewed when he came back to England in October. Anne
never seems to have taken her George very seriously. She was
a kind girl but sensible.

CHAPTER VII

Some very foolish influence rules the Pit
Not always kind to some or just to wit.

DRYDEN

Marking Time

ANNE'S BEAUTY had won popular favour in *The Pilgrim*, but for a matter of three years stagnation in her art persisted. Her agreeable figure and the sweetness of her voice, says one of Rich's staff, gave her preference over the other young actresses, and her salary was raised to a pound a week when one of her warmest admirers, the Duke of Bedford, spoke to the management. But she failed to impress the critics. Charles Gildon, in particular, unkindly described her and her rival, Jane Rogers, as rubbish that ought to be swept off the stage with the dust and filth.

During the first years of the century the brisk competition between Jane Rogers and Anne Oldfield persisted. They played small parts in a number of undistinguished new pieces with short runs as well as in the regular repertory. In Baker's farce *The Humour of the Age*, Anne played the kept mistress of Robert Wilks, to be married off at the end of the play to the low comedian. In Settle's opera *The Virgin Prophetess: or The Fate of Troy*, Jane played the title part of Cassandra, Anne for her good looks was Helen of Troy, and Wilks, Paris. No expense in production was spared and six white elephants (presumably of cardboard) made an appearance in the first act. In the last Anne had a spectacular and very final exit, leaping from the top of a tower into the flaming ruins of Troy. She spoke the prologue to Mrs Trotter's tragedy *The Unhappy Penitent*, in which as Anne of Brittany she had the satisfaction of winning away Jane's royal lover, Charles VII. In Higgons' *Generous Conqueror*, Anne's scene with Jane excited the critics' wrath for the effeminacy and weakness of the dialogue. ' I dare be hanged ', said Gildon forcibly, ' if Mrs Oldfield and Mrs Rogers could not have told the poet's mind in better language of their

own.' Vanbrugh's opinion of Anne's possibilities had declined
and he only gave her the part of a maid in his adaptation from
the French *The False Friend*. However, he entrusted to her the
epilogue:

> Indeed you men are fools and won't believe
> What dreadful things we women can forgive.

A forgotten but far from contemptible author, Charles
Burnaby, provided her with a good part in his *Modish Husband*.
She appears in boy's clothes in a midnight garden scene and
is mistaken by Mrs Verbruggen for Mr Wilks, to be carried off
into an arbour, from which embarrassment only feigned illness
extricates her. A less amusing effort of D'Urfey's *The Old Mode
and the New* had an hour's playing time cut after the first night,
which, says the chronicler sourly, must have been a great
improvement. Anne played the thankless part of daughter to
Sir Fumbler Oldmode, admirer of the fashions of Queen
Elizabeth's reign.

The best new play in which she and Mrs Rogers acted during
those years was *The Funeral*. This was Dick Steele's first effort
on the stage and he took the precaution of having a detail from
the regiment present at the first night to bear down opposition.
The epilogue:

> He knows he's numerous friends, nay knows they'll show it
> And for the fellow soldier save the poet.

declares a well-placed confidence in their services.

Steele, nicknamed The Black Knight or The Knave of Clubs
from his tallow complexion and sable wig, was, however
different in appearance, the George Bernard Shaw of the
eighteenth-century stage. Sharing a common country of origin,
both dramatists campaigned with the wit of their pens to
reform the abuses of their different worlds. Shaw attacked
exploited prostitution, bad housing, the evils of marriage and
the sentimentality of the contemporary stage. Steele assailed
duelling, brawling, mischiefs of the law, abuses in the army,
and the cynicism of contemporary comedy. Both, in spite of
verbosity and tendency to write essays in the middle of their
comedies, had a deep-seated sense of the theatre. After death

both became targets of little men who could never approach their talent.

In *The Funeral* the principal satire is directed at the burial customs of the great: ' the poor dead ', says the undertaker, ' are delivered into my custody, to be embalmed, slashed, cut and dragged about, not to do them honour but to satisfy the vanity or interest of their survivors.'

In Evelyn Waugh's *The Loved One* the technique of American morticians is parodied; *The Funeral* ridicules the sepulchral pomps of the Age of Reason. Mr Sable is addressing his mutes:

Where in the name of goodness have you all been? Have you brought the sawdust and tar for embalming? Have you the hangings and the sixpenny nails and my lord's coat-of-arms? . . . Well, come, you that are to be mourners in this house, put on your sad looks and walk by me that I may sort you. Ha, you! A little more upon the dismal! This fellow has a good mortal look; place him near the corpse. That wainscot face must be o'top of the stairs; that fellow almost in a fright at the entrance of the hall . . . let's have no laughing now on any provocation (*he makes faces*). Look yonder, that hale, well-looking puppy! You ungrateful scoundrel, did I not give you ten, then fifteen, now twenty shillings a week to be sorrowful?

Anne was miscast as Lady Sharlot, the more solemn of the two orphan wards of the deceased. Jane had a better part as the flippant orphan, Lady Harriet:

Oh! I hate a heart I can't break, when I please. What makes the value of dear china, but that it's so brittle?

In after years when the play was revived, Anne was given Lady Harriet's part and Jane took the widow, played in the original production by Mrs Verbruggen. An episode when Anne jumps out of the coffin, supposed to house her guardian, was stigmatized by the critics with some justice as reducing comedy to ' vilest farce '. ' This is surprising beyond all belief,' one of them said gravely, ' that a lady of her delicacy should be coffined up and kept close some hours without relief of one gasp of air. If that be comedy, I have done with the stage.' Still it was admitted that the town had received the piece with great applause, and the hope was expressed that the author would divert it with another play, next time more correct.

Lady Sharlot's suitor was played by Cibber, Lady Harriet's by Wilks. The time had not yet come when Mrs Oldfield and Wilks were the inevitable team in comedy.

'To beseech gracefully, to approach respectfully, to pity, to mourn, to love, are the places wherein Wilks may be said to shine with the utmost beauty' was Steele's tribute to his brother Irishman. Like Steele, Wilks was black and swarthy, but unlike him, tall and thin. He was the most generous, tender-hearted man of his age. Dr Johnson, who thought little of actors, describes him as humane, generous and candid, qualities which are rare, he says, in a profession which makes nearly every other man 'contemptuous, insolent, petulant, selfish and brutal'. His fellow professionals found Wilks rough-tongued and irritable, but Anne could always manage him.

Authors had cause to be grateful to Robert Wilks. He always knew his part and he never gagged. On the stage he could give a realistic impersonation of the graceful, arrogant, elegant beau of his day. Whatever he did, however trifling: taking off his gloves, taking out his watch, taking snuff, lolling on his cane, bore all the marks of breeding. Younger play-goers may remember in Gerald du Maurier a similar easy excellence. But, unlike the later actor, Wilks had the fault of fidgeting: 'his feet never stand still. He is like the pendulum of a clock, perpetually shuffling from one side to 'tother. That affected levity of his heels. . . .' David Garrick suffered from the same failing, as was pungently noted by George III.

Rehearsals of *The Funeral* were honoured by the presence of the Duke of Devonshire. Accompanying him must have come his intimate friend Sir Arthur Maynwaring. Thus casually may have occurred a first meeting with the man who was to change the whole tenor of Anne's life. She did not fall in love with him at first sight. He was thirty-four, fifteen years her elder; his looks did not set her heart beating. A long, narrow, oval face with heavy-lidded, supercilious eyes and a warm, sensual mouth had bitter lines that betrayed the satirist in him. A large, fair, bushy wig made his face seem even narrower. The wig was carefully curled and barbered, but his clothes proclaimed a deliberate negligence which was bound to repel Anne's elegance. What did he think of the rehearsal and her playing of Lady Sharlot? His companion, the Duke, whose wandering glances suggested more sophisticated tastes, proclaimed himself vastly moved by the innocence of the play. He expressed himself condescendingly in its favour. Arthur's smile was enigmatic. Then the two fine gentlemen sauntered airily out into the sunshine, leaving a whiff of ambergris behind them in the stuffy playhouse.

★　　　★　　　★

Next spring Anne was given a part in a new play by the Irish comedian, Dick Estcourt. It was called *The Fair Example* and, as Anne's virtue was that good example, the casting suggests that her affair with Farquhar had not tarnished the innocence that shone out of her eyes. Once again she played opposite Cibber, but Estcourt the actor had no literary style and Colley's and Anne's share of the comedy was dull and badly written. Unfairly, Cibber laid the blame of their failure to win laughs on her. It was a surprise when, at the end of the season, after another part in another play by Susan Centlivre, Rich raised her salary to fifty shillings.

Still Anne's career had slid into the doldrums. She had lost the impetus of her launch by Vanbrugh, who did not trouble to hide his disappointment in her. She was losing her struggle with the insufferable Jane Rogers, who persisted in getting the better parts. Her love affair with the coming man of the theatre had gone wrong. Not merely had it brought her no material advancement, but it had not developed her womanhood. Farquhar had not helped her art by precept (though she was loud in her praises of the vigorous horse sense of his *Discourse upon Comedy*) or by inspiration. Anne's heart was still virgin and her personality dormant.

D

CHAPTER VIII

The proverb holds that to be wise and love
Is hardly granted to the Gods above.
                                    DRYDEN

Passion

THE SUMMER of 1703 saw the turning point of Anne's life. It introduced her to a new stratum of society more civilized than the thrusting, cut-throat, intellectual Bohemianism of Drury Lane; it started her triumphal progress on the stage; it gave her a lover who was her emotional equal and whose affectionate help was devoted to mould her art; a lover who stuck to her until his death. All these blessings proceeded from a royal attack of the gout.

Queen Anne had come to the throne the previous year. Eighteen months of good living and ' she signified her pleasure that she intended to remove her Court from Windsor to Bath on Wednesday the 18th August '. Her principal physician Dr Edward Hannes accompanied her and was paid fifteen shillings a day travelling expenses. Her carver, Cornelius Tilburgh, only got five shillings less. Eight wagons carried the officers in attendance and another closed wagon was put at the disposal of the indispensable Sarah, Duchess of Marlborough. Lodging at Bath was hired for the Queen at the modest cost of four hundred and eighteen pounds.

For royal edification, the Reverend Mr Duke was chosen to preach at Bath Abbey on the last Sunday in August and arrangements were made to print his sermon. For the Court's more mundane tastes, the company of the Theatre Royal was ordered to accompany the expedition. The Queen herself took little interest in the play. She never went to the theatre and seldom commanded a performance at the Palace. To judge by her proclamations she regarded the stage as a menace. Complaints had been made, ran her frequent decrees, that many old, as well as new plays, were being acted which contained lines contrary to religion and good manners; while prologues, epilogues and songs were often indecent. On pain of Her Majesty's displeasure and the even more formidable risk of being silenced, companies were forbidden to act any play, new or old, that contained profane or indecent expressions. True, on her birthday Her Majesty's comedians, musicians and dancers were given an allowance of bread and wine, with candles and wax to light them, in a performance at Court. But this was traditional, for ever since light-minded King Charles's Restoration, the members of the Theatre Royal company had been put on the royal establishment and allowed ten yards of scarlet cloth each man and so much lace for liveries. But lest too much importance be attached to this honour, Queen Anne would notice that the Court ' ratt-killer ' wore also a livery and even a mourning livery on the death of her predecessor.

★   ★   ★

The summer move from Drury Lane to Bath was in every way the crisis of Anne's career. Poor Mrs Verbruggen, who was in possession of all the good parts that Anne was dying to play, had to be left behind. She had been peculiar for some time. One day, standing in the wings watching a performance of *Hamlet*, she had pushed aside the Ophelia of the moment and had gone on stage to give her own distressingly realistic version of that demented heroine. Rich gave orders she must be left behind and the company went to Bath without her. Soon afterwards she died giving birth to a daughter.

There was an immediate scramble among the ladies of the company for her parts. Anne's elbow was less sharp than Jane's, and only the part of Leonora in John Crowne's old play *Sir Courtly Nice* fell to her share. Crowne had been handed two Spanish plays by the late royal amateur, King Charles, with the order to turn them into an English comedy. When the first three acts were finished, the playwright read them aloud. His patron's criticism was characteristic: there was too little bawdy. A month later the King lay dying and the dramatist finished the play alone. The main character, the fop Sir Courtly Nice, was first played by Montford, first husband of Susan Verbruggen. ' The insipid, soft civility! ' rhapsodizes an eye-witness, ' the elegant and formal mien! The drawling delicacy

of voice, the stately flatness of his address, the empty eloquence
of his attitudes! ' This rôle now fell to Cibber to act before the
Court at Bath. Anne's part of Leonora was, in Colley's opinion,
one of good plain sense, not over-elegantly written. He was not
best pleased at having her to act opposite him. He had not
forgotten their failure in *The Fair Example* only a few weeks
earlier:

I had so cold an expectation from her abilities that she could
scarce prevail with me to rehearse with her the scenes with Sir
Courtly. However we ran them over with a mutual inadvertency.
I seemed careless, as concluding that any assistance I could give her
would be to little or no purpose. And she muttered out her words in
a sort of mifty manner at my low opinion of her.

But when the day for her performance came, Anne was anything
but ' mifty ':

She had just occasion to triumph over the error of my judgment
[says Cibber frankly,] by the amazement that her unexpected performance awakened me to. So forward, so sudden a step into nature
I had never seen.

Observe them in one of their scenes. Cibber looking, in the
words of one who knew him, like a pig half roasted with a voice
that might have been borrowed from the same suffering animal,
is pressing his unwanted attentions on Anne. She, ' tall, genteel,
well-shaped ', her body in lovely proportion, her hands significant in every motion and gesture, her voice musical and
entrancing, her pleasing, expressive features enlivened with the
large eyes which she would half shut, as she realized some fresh
idea for fooling the amorous Sir Courtly, is in the middle of her
sport:

Leonora	Can you hope for my heart, Sir Courtly, till I have some assurance of yours?
Sir Courtly	What assurance would your ladyship have?
Leonora	All manner. He that pretends to my heart must sigh and wait, and watch and pant, and fight and write – and kill himself!
Sir Courtly	All this have I done, madam, and ten thousand things more: drove by your windows a thousand times a day, sought you at the parks and the plays; was a constant

faithful attendant at all tragedies, for I presume your ladyship nauseates comedies?

Leonora   Oh foh!

Sir Courtly   They are so ill-bred and saucy with quality. Now at tragedies the house is all lined with beauty and then a gentleman may endure it. And I have gone, found not your ladyship there, drove home, killed myself with sighing – and then writ a song!

Leonora   Oh, Heavens! Sir Courtly, did you ever write a song upon me?

Sir Courtly   Above a thousand.

Leonora   Oh, there's nothing charms me like a song. For heaven's sake, the song, the song!

Sir Courtly   I've above forty here in a sweet bag. I'll show you the first I made upon your ladyship. 'Tis thought to be a pretty, foolish, soft song. Most ladies are very kind to it.
              (*he recites*) As I gazed unaware
                          On a face so fair . . .

Leonora   Oh, Sir Courtly!

Sir Courtly   Your cruel eye
              Lay watching by
              To snap my heart,
              Which you did with such art
              That away with it you ran
              To my ruin and grief:
              Stop thief! Stop thief!

Leonora   Oh fine! Oh fine!

Sir Courtly   (*complacently*) That ' stop thief', madam, is pretty novel.

Leonora   Oh delicate! I'm charmed. I'm lost! (*pretending to recover herself*) Fie, what have I said?

Sir Courtly   What makes me the happiest of creatures (*he tries to take her hand*).

Leonora   (*removing it*) I only rally. Away! The song again, the song! I'll have nothing but the song. Is there no tune to it?

Sir Courtly   One of my own composing.

Leonora   That accomplishment too? Heavens, how fine a gentleman is this!

Sir Courtly   Oh, madam, how proud you make me.

Leonora   Oh dear! How I betray myself! Foolish creature, no more, no more. The tune, the tune!

Sir Courtly   I always humour my words with my air. So I make the

voice shake at the last line, in imitation of a man that
runs after a thief. (*sings*) Sto-ho-ho-hop thief!

Leonora   Oh delicate! Cannot I hear it? Sto-ho-ho- (*bursts out
laughing*) Ha! ha! ha!

' In this part ', ran Cibber's verdict, ' she surprised me into
an opinion of her having all the innate powers of a good actress.
And ', he continues, ' what made her performance more valuable was that I knew it proceeded all from her own understanding, untaught and unassisted by any one more experienced
actor.'

He was right. Anne's startling progress was due to no
coaching she had received from any member of the profession.
She had fallen deeply in love.

Beside the communicating spark that defies all definition,
the little ex-barmaid demanded from the man she was to fall
in love with, the two qualifications of intelligence and breeding.
They were perhaps easier to discover in one person in her
century than in ours. In Arthur Maynwaring – wit, satirist and
man of fashion – she found what she was looking for. For his
part, he ' selected her from all the Fair Part of Creation that
graces our Isle, to be his Bosom Companion and share his Joys
and Cares '. In the thirty-five years of his life, he had had long
enough to make this selection: in the aristocratic circles of his
birth, for a wife, and in the taverns and greenrooms, for a
mistress. He was born at Ightfield, Shropshire, where his family
had lived since the fifteenth century. His grandfather, also Sir
Arthur, had some claim to remembrance as the lover of the
Mrs Turner who was intimately concerned in the poisoning of
Sir Thomas Overbury. (She tried out the aphrodisiacs designed
for the Earl of Essex on Sir Arthur and he was said to have
been so affected that he rode fifteen miles through a thunder-
storm to visit their contriver.) His namesake was educated at
Shrewsbury Grammar School and the House. Four years'
sojourn at the latter establishment and the tuition of a future
Bishop of Bristol did not avail to procure him a degree. He was
called to the Bar in the year of the Glorious Revolution, in
which event he ranked as a Tory and Jacobite. One of his
uncles, Sir Francis Cholmondeley, got into trouble over his
politics. Arthur was rather flippant: ' 'Tis true my uncle is in

the Tower,' he wrote, ' but 'tis his own fault, for he may come out if he will. He has indeed some scruple of conscience, but that, they tell him, is the disease of a Quaker and not to be indulged in by any true Protestant.' Arthur's political convictions were not deep and an introduction to Lord Somers and other Whig supporters of William III easily induced him to turn his coat. His father, with whom he had been living in London, died when he was twenty-five, leaving him an encumbered estate of eight hundred pounds a year. He first mortgaged and then sold Ightfield. ' He loved gaming a little in his younger days and particularly bowling. He used to bowl high with the Duke of Devonshire and other persons of quality. It has been said that he was no loser by his play, but as he was a man of strict honour, one must impute it to his luck.' (Skill was not, it seems, in question.) In his younger years he drank pretty freely. His wit was very formidable to ' coxcombs and pretenders '. Indeed, he would have had fewer enemies if he had not made merry at their expense. He was one of the chief ornaments of the Kit-cat Club and was said by Pope to have been the ruling man there in all conversations.

This celebrated Whig club was founded at the beginning of the century with the ostensible object of encouraging literature and the fine arts. But it measured talent, said Matthew Prior, by the unerring balance of party. Of its founder Jacob Tonson, the Tory Dryden wrote:

I am the founder of your loved Kit-cat,
A club that gives direction to the State;
'Twas there we first instructed all our youth
To talk profane and laugh at sacred truth;
We taught them how to toast and rhyme and ' bite ',
To sleep away the day and drink away the night.

The club met once a week, originally near Temple Bar, at the house of a pastry-cook, it is said, whose name was Christopher Catt. The *Fountain* in the Strand, the *Upper Flask* at Hampstead, and the secretary Jacob Tonson's house at Barn Elms, were later *rendezvous*. Each member in turn was master of the feast. Toasts were drunk to reigning beauties and their names were scratched with a diamond on the glasses. Verse, largely obscene, was entered in a commonplace book. Kneller was a member and painted the portraits of his brother members in the Kit-cat dimensions required to fit Tonson's dining-room.

Beside a bevy of Whig aristocrats with the Duke of Marlborough at their head, men of letters like Congreve, Steele, Addison, Vanbrugh and Garth were members, and it says something for Maynwaring's magnetism that he passed for a great genius among them. This reputation has not survived the beauty of the ladies the club toasted. It rested, it seems, on his conversation. It is recorded that his learning was without pedantry, and his wit without affectation. He was fond of literature and made verse translations of Horace and Ovid, and prose translations of Cicero. He wrote epilogues and prologues to plays, and political satires in verse and prose. He was an enthusiast for Italian opera and took pleasure in playing the airs on his spinet. To-day, in spite of a contemporary opinion that his works would be ' a standard of good writing as long as wit, humour and elegance have any value in our Island,' he is forgotten and his writings seem unreadable.

A bit of one of his verse translations may be quoted, for it may give some idea how Anne Oldfield looked to him. It is from Ovid's *Art of Love*, ' translated into English by several eminent hands ', and the episode called *The Court of Love* is, according to a note in Pope's handwriting, the work of Anne's lover.

The author is summoned to appear before the Court of Venus, charged with despising her votaries. He is taken into the presence of the goddess:

> Her golden Hair, dishevell'd, crisp and long
> In easie Curls around her Shoulders hung.

He pleads guilty and submits himself to her will:

> Yours be the Choice, I only wish to find
> A Faithful Mistress, beautiful and kind
> With whom in Pleasure I may spend my Life;
> My Mistress, Empress – anything but Wife.

Venus produces the girl she has chosen for him. Did not Anne sit for the portrait, all allowance being made for translator's licence?

Her Head is round and flaxen is her Hair,
Her Eyebrows darker, but her Forehead fair,
Straight is her Nose; her Eyes like Emeralds bright,
Her well-made Cheeks are lovely red and white,
Her Hands are snowy white and small her Waist
And what is yet untold is sure the best. . . .

The poet takes an oath: ' To love one Fair unchangedly till
Death ', and all is leading to a happy climax, when: ' Rapture
wak'd me and the Vision fled.'

Arthur caught his first sight of Anne, it has been supposed,
at a rehearsal of *The Funeral*. He followed up his advantage
nightly in wings and Greenroom at Drury Lane. Then came
the move of Court and players to Bath. Maynwaring went too.
The mild summer air of Bath ripened friendship to love. There
was also the stimulus of a rival. ' Bedford's pretty Duke,
wounded by a look ', had, not many months earlier, won
Anne a rise in salary. He was now in hot pursuit. One morning
he called at her lodging. She was out but he left a letter, with
what he fancied must prove an unanswerable argument. It was
a settlement for life of six hundred pounds a year. This was no
small temptation to a fifty shillings a week actress with several
indigent relations. Getting wind of this bid, Arthur Maynwaring
called the next day and pressed Anne to yield to his passionate
importunities. Anne ' candidly confessed her regard for him,
but told him he was an unlucky fellow for that something had
happened the day before '. Arthur had his suspicions. He begged
her to explain. She was silent and tearful. A little later he called
again. She told him of the settlement and added, laughing, that
she had returned the deed to the donor. As Arthur had inherited an encumbered estate of eight hundred pounds a year
and Anne was spurning an offer of six hundred for life to be
enjoyed on a ducal pillow, the veteran actor Charles Macklin
cannot be said to have exaggerated when he said that her love
affairs were always those of sentiment rather than interest.

She had her reward. From that day until his death nine years
later, Arthur Maynwaring loved her with ' a dear and generous
passion '. She was no less infatuated, for, says his biographer
dryly: ' Each loved with a passion that could hardly have been
stronger had it been both her and his first love.'

There is a haunting little song in the Crowne play that Anne and Arthur heard many a time as they stood hand-in-hand in the wings:

> Oh be kind, my dear, be kind
> While our loves and we are young!
> We shall find, we shall find
> Time will change the face or mind,
> Youth will not continue long;
> Oh be kind, my dear, be kind. . . .

Anne was abundantly kind.

In return Maynwaring's passionate affection gave her a faith in man which her casual contacts behind the scenes, and George Farquhar's amiable polygamy, had hitherto done little to foster. Besides its psychological effect on her art and her entrance under its guidance into full womanhood, she had the benefit of a taste in artistic matters which the contemporary world qualified as ' exquisite and refined '. Nobody, it said, understood acting better than Maynwaring and nobody took more delight to help her excel. He wrote prologues and epilogues for her to speak, and rehearsed her in them. There can be little doubt that Anne's sensational leap forward when she played Leonora, owed much to Arthur's affectionate coaching.

CHAPTER IX

A silk suit which cost me much money and I pray God to
make me able to pay for it.

S. PEPYS

Back to Earth

ANNE WAS NOT the only member of the company for whom
destiny knocked that summer at Bath. It was Miss Campion's
good fortune, it is stated, to be honoured with the friendship
of Arthur Maynwaring's partner on the bowling green, William
Duke of Devonshire. Mary Anne Campion was in her teens.
She captivated the sixty-three-year-old Duke (more indeed by
her singing and dancing than by her acting) so desperately,
that he persuaded her to leave the stage and consecrate her
charm to him. Their happiness was not of long duration. ' She
was taken off in her bloom by a hectic fever under which she
languished but four months, being but nineteen years of age.
Her endowments, both of mind and body, are very elegantly
delineated in the inscription upon a very neat marble tablature
erected to her memory by his Grace ' in a Buckinghamshire
church:

> Resting in Peace, her mortal part here lies,
> But her immortal soul assumes the skies;
> Her lovely form with every grace conjoined
> Illustrated the virtues of her mind.
> Though meanly born, her morals were sincere
> And such as the most noble blood might wear . . .
> Sacred to her most dear remains be't known
> His Grace of Devon consecrates this stone.

During her lifetime the Duke gave her a prayer book in
which he wrote on a blank page twelve ' remarkable ' verses of
Dryden recommending a plan of natural religion. He was not
the last old gentleman to combine sensuality with sancti-
moniousness.

★ ★ ★

Anne's standing was better than Miss Campion's. She had not

59

been ' taken off the stage ' and had not subsided into the ranks
of the *demi-monde*. Thanks to her natural wit, she could mix
with the great on something like equal terms. The day had not
yet come when she was accepted by wives and sisters, but
Maynwaring's circle was predominantly male and he appre-
ciated the bohemian world of theatre and letters. It was not yet
the fashion for actresses to marry well. The most a nobleman or
a man of gentle birth could honourably do was to take a player
into keeping. Martin Folkes, President of the Royal Society,
son of a bencher of Gray's Inn and of a knight's daughter, was
the first man of any standing to take a wife from the stage.
About 1714 he married Lucretia Bradshaw, whose name
appears in many a Farquhar and Congreve cast. The fashion
he started, quickly spread to the aristocracy. Some fifteen years
later the eccentric Earl of Peterborough announced a secret
wedding to the actress singer, Anastasia Robinson. Another
fifteen years and the Duke of Bolton, after a long wait for his
Duchess to die, espoused Lavinia Fenton, original Polly of *The
Beggar's Opera*. It became almost a rule for peers to marry the
' Polly ' of the moment, as Lord Essex exemplified with Miss
Stephens and the poetic Lord Thurlow with Miss Bolton. Anne
was just too old to benefit by this trend towards stage marriages.
The tradition of her day dated back to Imperial Rome, whose
actresses were classed with prostitutes and forbidden by law to
marry patricians. There was, as late as the days of George II,
the case of a lady of title, ' whose female indiscretions had
occasioned her family to abandon her '. She turned to the stage
for a living. Her relatives took the trouble to beg the management not to accept her, lest her engagement should ' add fresh
scandal to her former dishonour '. Nor was the social standing
of male actors much higher. True, their position was better
than in Louis XIV's France where Molière, as an actor, was
refused burial in consecrated ground. The King was supposed
to have asked the Archbishop of Paris how far consecrated
ground reached. On being told about eight feet, ' Let, therefore, Molière's grave be dug twelve foot deep ', replied the
Grand Monarch easily. Even in England John Dennis defied
anyone to name a single great actor of his time who had had a
generous education, by which, he explained, he meant a train-

ing in the arts and sciences. ' Nor do I know ', he continued, 'of any one great actor, since the establishment of the stage, who had extraordinary parts. Shakespeare indeed had great parts, but he was not a great actor. Otway and Lee had both education and parts, but they were wretched actors.'

As late as the end of the century, it took the intervention of the Lord Chief Justice to get Arthur Murphy, the playwright, permission to enter his name for Lincoln's Inn. After a youth spent on the stage, he had already been refused admission by the Middle Temple. James Boswell was conscious of paradoxical daring, when he said that people seemed to forget the profession of a player was as laborious as of law, physic or divinity. When he added that there were very few ladies outside the walls of a convent, whose time was so regularly allocated and whose minds were so innocently occupied as actresses, he could only hope to raise a smile.

This was sixty years on, and on the day that Anne returned from Bath to London under the protection of Sir Arthur Maynwaring, such breadth of mind was unthinkable. To meet her bills, for Anne, alas, had expensive tastes, Maynwaring abandoned an unproductive practice at the Bar. With the help of the Duke of Somerset (Anne's circle was now very ducal) he secured a post as Commissioner of Customs. Normally there would be pickings, but no man had a greater contempt for money than Maynwaring. A candidate for a job as tide-waiter once left on him a letter, urging his claims and underlining them with a purse of fifty guineas. When his case came up, the Commissioner was unworldly enough to throw the purse on the table, declaring that as long as he could prevent it, the candidate should not have that, or any other, post. Instead of taking the easy way to fortune, he applied himself to figures and to learning his job, and soon earned the reputation of being the most able man on the Board.

Anne was not the woman to let a love affair, however absorbing, conflict with her ambition to become a great actress. She had also to make both ends meet. She soon plunged into the whirl of the new season. Steele gave her the part of the heroine Victoria in his second comedy *The Lying Lover*. The second girl Penelope was played by Jane Rogers and the stage

quarrels of the couple (played no doubt with conviction) make
the liveliest scenes in the play. Wilks acted the name part, with
Cibber, his friend. Though the play ran six nights, it was
stamped as a failure and has only once since been revived. The
seeds of its mortality were inherent in the author's benevolent
theories. His design was to banish all entertainment which did
not proceed from ' simplicity of mind, good-nature, friendship
and honour '. The early eighteenth-century playhouse was no
place for his ' honest ambition to attempt a comedy which
might be no improper entertainment in a Christian common-
wealth '. In fact the piece is not nearly as dull as these pious
aspirations suggest. The hero, in the author's own words, makes
false love, gets drunk and kills his man; in the fifth act he
awakens from his debauch with compunction and remorse.
With the blue pencilling of some of this compunction and the
omission of some appalling blank verse, a very tolerable entertainment might merit revival even at this late date, when there
is said to be a shortage of actable plays.

Next year, the glorious year of Blenheim and of the capture
of Gibraltar, saw Anne's first appearance in a tragic lead. In
John Banks's tragedy *The Albion Queens* she played no meaner
character, nor one more defiant of success, than Mary Queen
of Scots. The piece had been written and published twenty
years before, but ever since the demise of Charles I, plays
featuring the execution of monarchs were discouraged, and its
public performance had been banned. Now a Court admirer
of the work (is the finger of Maynwaring to be discerned?)
succeeded in getting the ban lifted. High-brow critics condemned Banks's work as bad poetry ' written in a barren,
barbarous style '. But he wrote three effective historical dramas.
Besides Mary Queen of Scots, his *Vertue Betray'd* presented the
case of the ill-starred Anne Bullen, and *The Unhappy Favourite*
that of the no less unfortunate Earl of Essex. All three ' had the
good fortune to please the fair sex, which had some difficulty
to refrain from tears, whenever these plays were given '. The
truth was, whatever his faults of style, Banks could write a
simple plot and provide a good acting vehicle, especially
when he had an actress like Anne to draw tears from the
Boxes. It is indeed a thankless task to sift the less bad from

the ruck of tragedies that delighted the century's audiences. Lady Mary Wortley Montagu was inspired to write an epilogue for Mrs Oldfield to speak at the end of the tragedy. True to the fashion of the day, it was designed to relax the tension:

> Light as the air and fleeting as the wind,
> Whatever poets write and lovers vow,
> Beauty, what poor omnipotence hast thou! . . .
> If you will love, love like Eliza then,
> Love for the moment like those traitors men. . . .
> Hear, but be faithful to your interest still,
> Secure your wants, then fool with whom you will.

Anne's instinct for comedy could be relied on to make every point in an epilogue of this nature, but of what she did with her exacting part as Mary Stuart there is little record. Two lines of indifferent verse:

> But when our Scottish Mary was her part . . .
> Our stage became a sea of briny tears

testify to the pathos she was able to extract. This first performance of a shelved play was carefully staged. Prices were raised to meet the cost of new costumes for Anne and new scenery, but its notable success testifies to twenty-year-old Anne's growing powers and to her lover's unofficial direction. In spite of his help, Anne was still dissatisfied with her equipment for tragedy. ' I hate to have a page dragging my tail about! ' she exclaimed in protest at the tragic convention of the day. ' Why do they not give Porter these parts? She can put on a better tragedy face than I can! '

There was never the jealousy of Mary Porter that Anne felt for Jane Rogers. Mary had been left fatherless at an early age and was put to act in a booth at Bartholomew Fair by an unsympathetic mother. Playing the Fairy Queen, she had been discovered by Mrs Barry, who gave her her early training. Seeing many years later the finished product, the elder actress, conscious of the impermanence of dramatic fame, was heard to exclaim, ' Dear Porter, I shall never die, while you live! ' Three years before the production of the Mary Stuart play, Mary attracted attention as Jessica in *The Jew of Venice*, Lord Lansdowne's adaptation of *The Merchant of Venice*, whereby his lordship's judicious pen was considered to have preserved all that was valuable in the original. Mrs Porter was fair and tall and had a good figure. That ' Nature had been niggard to her in voice and face ' perhaps explains Anne's lack of envy. Mary was no comedienne and even in tragedy, complaint was made that her coarse, rough voice was apt to become monotonous in a cadenced, chanting delivery. That was a fault of the day, and in passionate scenes she could rise to great heights. Dr Johnson (for she survived to die in poverty in the second half of the century) declared that he had never seen her equalled ' in the vehemence of rage '. At one time she lived near Hendon and, fortified with a book and a brace of horse pistols, used to drive home after the play in a chaise. Ignorant of her habits, a highwayman had the temerity to hold her up. Finding one of her pistols presented at his head, he told a hard-luck story that he was driven to such courses by the distress of his family. The sympathetic tragedienne lowered the pistol and offered him ten guineas for their relief. Poetic justice was not done her, for on whipping up her horse, the animal swerved and upset the chaise, dislocating Mrs Porter's thigh bone. Ever after, she had to act leaning on a stick. In her goodness of heart, she felt no resentment against the cause of her accident. Hobbling about, she checked the highwayman's story; finding it true, she raised a subscription of sixty pounds to help his family.

★   ★   ★

Anne's position at Drury Lane was now well enough established to provide her with a regular benefit, a privilege reserved for the more notable performers. Hers was granted at the end of March before takings had begun to decline. (From the end of spring until the season closed in June or July attendance at the playhouses fell off.) This year Mrs Oldfield's benefit performance, which was billed as at the desire of several persons of quality, consisted of a rather curious treble bill. The first item was a two-act farce of Cibber's called *The School Boy*, followed by the two doctors' scenes in the last act of a recent adaptation by Mrs Centlivre of Molière's *Le Médecin malgré Lui*. Interspersed were ' several musical entertainments by the late Mr H.

Purcell '. The whole was enlivened with dancing by The Devonshire Girl, Monsieur de Ruell, Monsieur Cherrier and Mrs Mayers.

The School Boy was a rather crude bit of humour dug out of a longer play of Cibber's which had failed at Drury Lane seven years before. The principal interest lies in a not very edifying rivalry between Old Rakish and his son, Major Rakish.

Of all the vices this town affords and, Heaven bless the reformers, there's still a pretty considerable stock, I can't keep one for myself [protests the gallant major]. My father out-drinks me, out-whores me, out-swears me, out-wits me and, which I'll never forgive him, he out-lives me too.

He has to admit that Old Rakish has recently raised his allowance; but since he makes him play picquet and ' bagamon ' with him, and wins it all back, nothing is gained. Both father and son seek the hand of the wealthy widow, Lady Manlove. Her pretty maid Lettice (played by Anne Oldfield) and her loutish son Johnny (played by the low comedian) are about to embark on a secret marriage. In a series of intrigues, Major Rakish stops the wedding, pairs off his father with Lady Manlove and gets his allowance raised.

The Purcell music would be an agreeable variant. The pieces played were the prologue to *The Indian Queen*, the sacrifice in *King Arthur* and the masque from *Timon of Athens*. There was a grand cockfight that day for ten guineas a battle and two hundred pounds the odd battle, between the gentlemen of Essex and Cambridge and the gentlemen of London and Surrey. Many a seat at Anne's benefit must have been left empty, thanks to this rival attraction.

E

CHAPTER X

.... The slope of faces from the floor to th' roof
Reflected in an universal grin.
                                        COWPER

Leading Lady

AT LAST THE summer heat announced the end of the season and Anne and her lover were free to escape from the stench of London. Looking about for some seclusion for their passion, their choice of a love-nest fell, not unambitiously, on Windsor Castle. There was housed a broad-minded friend of Arthur's, Mr John Sewell, Chapter Clerk to the Dean of Windsor and Treasurer of Eton College. He readily put his quarters at their disposal.

Another visitor at the house of this tolerant cleric was also intimately connected with the stage. He came bringing an half-finished play in his pocket. So far, Anne had had to be thankful to accept any part she was offered, either in new plays or from the current repertory. Why, urged her visitor, should not she now take a step forward and appear in a part specially written for her?

Colley Cibber was the more or less successful actor-playwright who unrolled these plans to Anne and Arthur. He was the son of a sculptor father from Schleswig, who executed the twin figures of Delirium and Melancholia that enlivened the façade of Bedlam:

> Where o'er the gates by his famed father's hand
> Great Cibber's brazen, brainless brothers stand!

After bearing arms for William of Orange, young Cibber found that his father had ruined himself gambling and was having to leave a debtors' gaol every morning to carve the reliefs on the base of the Monument. Colley went on the stage. His hatchet face, with its ' pensive, yet protruded, sharpness ' and his natural bent, qualified him for parts of fops and decrepit old men. Finding no characters to his taste (someone

66

said that the beaux of those days displayed the stateliness of the peacock rather than the mid-century pertness of the lapwing) he wrote himself the part of Sir Novelty Fashion in *Love's Last Shift*,[1] which the Lord Chamberlain of the day declared to be the best first play he remembered. Latter-day critics, who can never have gone to the lengths of reading the work, are apt to pronounce it the forerunner of the moral crop of comedies that succeeded the licence of the Reformation and Revolution. In fact, it is vigorous, bawdy stuff, marred by hurried writing, ending with the sudden conversion of the hero after, as he admits in the epilogue, ' he had been lewd for above four acts '. Congreve said with some justice that there were many lines in the play which were *like* wit, without being witty, as when Sir Novelty says:

Pray madam, how do I look to-day? What, cursedly I warrant? With a more hellish complexion than a stale actress in the morning? I don't know madam, 'tis true the town does talk of me indeed, but the Devil take me, in my mind I am a very ugly fellow.

Or again:

All young fellows hate the name of fop as women do the name of whore. But i'Gad they both love the pleasure of being so!

Witty or no, the play was a great success and Vanbrugh borrowed Sir Novelty (ennobling him into Lord Foppington) for a sequel *The Relapse*. Cibber, launched as a dramatist, tried again. His second attempt, *Woman's Wit*, from which he later extracted Anne's first benefit farce *The School Boy*, was a failure. The reasons he himself gave for its miscarriage are: first, his prevalent fault, too great haste in writing; secondly, that he had been compelled to contrive a plot, whereas the idea for *Love's Last Shift* came to him spontaneously, ' the kindly product of my fancy '. In all the two dozen plays which he was to commit in the eighty-six years of his life, plot was his unfailing difficulty. He usually found a solution in borrowing from some previous writer's work. But for the play which he had now in his head for Anne Oldfield, the dominating situation came to

[1] The Duchess of Bolton was once asked by King George I, who had no English, what play she had patronized at Drury Lane. The Duchess, who had little more French, answered, ' La dernière chemise d'amour, Sire! '

hand ready-made from real life. How this happened is a not unentertaining story.

It begins with Colonel Henry Brett of Sandywell Park, Gloucestershire. Expensive tastes led to the mortgaging of that estate and carried their possessor to London about the time of the first night of Cibber's first play. Drawn to Drury Lane and its Greenroom by the charms of the ' nymphs ' and even more by the fascination of a full-bottomed wig Cibber wore playing Sir Novelty, the soldier struck up a friendship with the actor over a bottle and soon the pair became bosom friends.

Colonel Brett's business in London lay not exclusively with the nymphs of the Theatre Royal. He was also pursuing the acquaintance of Anne, divorced wife of Lord Macclesfield. She made up for a sallow complexion, thick lips and a smallpox-pitted skin, with a beautiful figure and a fortune of twenty-five thousand pounds. The latter, he felt, ' would disencumber him of the world and make him easy for life '. He had already made an entry into the lady's sympathies as a brace of bailiffs arrested him for debt under her window. This informal introduction was followed by a more regular presentation by Sir Thomas Skipworth, one of the Patentees of Drury Lane.

One night Cibber found Brett dallying behind the scenes and admonished him for wasting his time. The lady of his choice was to remain in London, he well knew, only another three weeks. Brett had an excuse ready. His linen was too soiled to allow him to be seen in society. Cibber, who was dressed to go on the stage, took him into his dressing-room, where they exchanged shirts. Ten days later the banns were called for Colonel Henry Brett and Anne, lately Countess of Macclesfield.

The actor's good offices gave him the run of the Brett household and the Colonel introduced him to company to which he had not hitherto found access. This was very gratifying to Cibber, who in after life was inordinately proud of his admission to White's, then not a club but a coffee house. The dialogue of his plays began, he flattered himself, to take on a polish. And the central situation for the play he wanted to write was given him by an incident he witnessed, or was told of, in the Brett *ménage*. One afternoon Anne Brett had returned unexpectedly home to find her husband and her housemaid comfortably asleep in two armchairs exhausted by their recent activities. Eager not to disturb the Colonel's repose and anxious about a draught from the window, the tolerant woman tip-toed across the room and tied her scarf round her peccant husband's neck. Its discovery when he awoke was the only sign Brett ever had that Anne knew anything of his lapse.

Perhaps her own past had taught her not to set the standard of married fidelity too high. Before being divorced by Lord Macclesfield, she had borne first an illegitimate daughter and then a son to Lord Rivers. During her second *accouchement* she had worn a mask to protect her identity from the curious eyes of doctor and midwife. The daughter died. The son lived, if the story may be believed, to become the poet and playwright Richard Savage, immortalized by the pen and friendship of Doctor Johnson.

★　　★　　★

Even now that Cibber had found his central situation for *The Careless Husband*, the writing of the play did not progress. The character of Lady Betty Modish, the frivolous, good-hearted, dress-mad butterfly was hard to cast. Mrs Bracegirdle, who would have been suitable, was busy with Betterton in his Lincoln's Inn Fields company. Susan Verbruggen, who would have been ideal, was dead. Then Anne Oldfield showed him at Bath what she could do.

Cibber took the two acts he had finished to the lodging of the benevolent Chapter Clerk at Windsor. He found a good audience in Arthur and Anne. They laughed heartily at the story of Anne Brett's husband and her housemaid. They agreed that Bob Wilks would be perfect casting for that Careless Husband. They applauded Cibber's vivid portrayal of the rôle he had written for himself, the obligatory fop. And Anne's expressive eyes brightened when he began to read Lady Betty Modish's lines, a part that he vowed would fit her like a glove. . . .

Cibber went home to finish his play. By late autumn it was ready to go into rehearsal. It was billed in the daily Press as the first new play of the season, alongside advertisements for escaped slaves, stolen dogs and horses, cures for venereal

disease, oysters at three shillings a barrel, glass eyes, white port
at five shillings a gallon, ' one sweet monkey that whistles like
a bird ', false teeth ' so firm and exact as to be ate on ', dream
books and books on ' the whole art of amour '. No publicity
trick was spared to draw attention. In his dedication to the
Duke of Argyll, Cibber declared that the greater part of the
dialogue was borrowed from His Grace's own manner of conversing. He put rumours about that the Duke had actually
written the play. Its familiarity with the manners of the great
proved it. When this attribution was too much for the public
to swallow, he hinted that Sir Arthur Maynwaring was the
author. Much of the action of the play took place in Lady
Betty's lodgings at Windsor (with lines like ' Well, child, how
does Windsor air agree with you? '), and gossip ran the rounds
that none but Anne, holiday-making there with her lover, had
sat for the picture. Her own conversation was reflected, they
said, in the dialogue. What could be more likely than that
Maynwaring, not Cibber, had noted those jewels? In point of
fact the nearest Arthur came to a hand in the authorship was
with a prologue designed for the sixth day (the second of the
author's benefits), ' written by a person of quality ' but never
spoken. It begins with the sound sentiment, ' A paying nation
hates the fighting trade ', and in its championship of Marlborough in the year of Blenheim,

> Minerva guides our general to Fame,
> Mild in the camp, by no success made vain,
> Whose generous soul seeks only to restrain
> Unbounded tyranny . . .

echoes the Whig point of view that Maynwaring now professed.
   How far Anne's own words are mirrored in Lady Betty's
bons mots it is less easy to tell. A contemporary bears witness that
' all who had the pleasure of her acquaintance, asserted that the
dramatic pencil had delineated the real character of Mrs
Oldfield under the imaginary one of Lady Betty. She was
beautiful without artifice and her address and conversation,
engaging without affectation '. As, however, the whole point
of the characterization of Lady Betty is that she was supremely
artificial and her every word highly affected, the point is hard

to take. The author of the play put his obligations clearly enough:

Whatever favourable reception this comedy has met with from the public [wrote Cibber], it would be unjust in me not to place a large share to the account of Mrs Oldfield, not only for the uncommon excellence of her action but even from her personal manner of conversing. There are many sentiments in the character of Lady Betty Modish that I may almost say were originally her own, or only dressed with a little more care than when they negligently fell from her lively humour. Had her birth placed her in a higher rank of life, she had certainly appeared in reality, what in this play she only excellently acted, an agreeably gay woman of quality, a little too conscious of natural attractions.

As often happens with compliments passed by one player on another, there is a sting in the tail. Anne was a lovely woman and she knew it. She was also a witty one, though Pope, who never liked her, described her style of conversation as *Oldfieldismos*, writing the word in Greek characters to make his criticism more weighty. But all her recorded sayings are witty, tactful and wise. If Lady Betty Modish's pose was really Mrs Oldfield's, to the jaundiced eye it may have expressed something a little precious and coy. But how much was due to Cibber's interpositions? Let Lady Betty speak for herself:
' At this rate you would rather be thought beautiful than good? ' asks Lady Easy, without originality, of her;

As I had rather command than obey [replies Lady Betty]. The wisest homely woman can't make a man of sense a fool, but the veriest fool of a beauty can make an ass of a statesman. So that in short, I can't see a woman of spirit has any business in the world but to dress and make the men like her.

On her elegant toilets Mrs Oldfield was beginning to build a reputation, and her voice may be heard when Lady Betty discourses on her new scarf from London:

'Tis all extravagance in mode and fancy. My dear, I believe there's six thousand yards of edging in it. Then such an enchanting slope from the elbow; something so new, so lively, so noble, so coquette and charming!

Later she waxes philosophical:

Constancy shall be the mark of age and ugliness; virtue a jest;
we'll rally discretion out of doors, lay gravity at our feet, bid only
love, freelove, disorder, liberty and pleasure be our standing
principles.

But that is after her conversion, when she has begged forgiveness from her suitor for all the ' giddy woman's slights ' she has
inflicted, and has declared her utter detestation of any gallantry
that has been paid her ' to his uneasiness '. The man she has
been flirting with is, of course, Cibber's fop, with his entertaining clutter of oaths: ' Run me through, madam ', ' Sunburn
me, sir ', ' Let me blood ', ' Strike me stupid '; and true to the
vanity of actor-playwrights he comes *deus ex machina* at the
finish and guides the play to a happy issue.

The piece lacks action. There is only one good situation: the
Anne Brett incident of the Steinkirk scarf round the sleeping
husband's neck, which originally set Cibber's dramatic juices
to work. The rest of the plot, the reformation of the careless
husband and the conversion of flighty Lady Betty Modish, are
machine-made. But on 7 December 1704 the play, after a
shaky start (' 'Twas at first a moot point whether *The Careless
Husband* should live or die, but the houses it has since filled have
reproached the former coldness of its auditors '), picked up and
scored a smash hit. It was given nine nights running and
fourteen times in the first two months, an outstanding success
for those days. Anne Oldfield's reputation for comedy was safe.
From that day till her death, a quarter of a century later, she
never looked back.

The play was repeated in the new year, reinforced by several
Italian sonatas on the violin by Signor Gasperini and dancing
by Monsieur du Ruell. On 2 January, Mrs Cross (whose excursion to France with a baronet gave Anne her start on the
boards) returned after an absence from the stage of five years
to sing a pastoral dialogue with Mr Leveridge, as makeweight.

The stage was threatening one of its periodic slumps and the
discovery of the comic genius of Mrs Oldfield came just in time.
As to-day, when the competition of television, successor to the
rivalry of the motion picture, is stated to be the ruin of the

living theatre, so at the beginning of the eighteenth century the stage was ' not only pestered with tumblers and ropedancers from France but likewise dancing masters and dancing dogs; shoals of Italian squallers were daily imported and the Drury Lane Company almost broke '. To compete with the rival house in Lincoln's Inn Fields, where Rich was only deterred from bringing an elephant on the stage by the protests of his stage carpenter, the Theatre Royal had to supplement legitimate comedies with the talent of the celebrated Mr Clinch of Barnet who gave an ' imitation of an organ with three voices, the double curtel and the bells, the huntsman with his horn and pack of dogs, and an old woman of fourscore nursing her grandchild, all which he does with his mouth upon the open stage. Next a gentleman ' (a Mr Henry) ' will perform several mimic entertainments on the ladder. First he stands on the top rung with a bottle in one hand and a glass in the other and drinks a health, then plays several tunes on the violin.'

A couple of days before *The Careless Husband* was produced a series of advertisements in the *Flying Post* show how keen was the competition. In the Concert Room in Villiers Street, at the desire of several persons of quality, select entertainments of vocal and instrumental music were to start at eight o'clock. For lower brows, there was the first appearance at the *Blue Boar* in Fleet Street of the High German professor who had been born without hands or arms. Nevertheless ' he writes very fair with his mouth in five languages; threads a fine needle with his feet; shaves, dresses and undresses; beats a drum, fires a gun, etc. Admission one shilling, beginning at six p.m.' At the *White Horse* next door was to be seen, at any time of day, a little black, hairy pigmy from the deserts of Araby with a natural ruff of hair about his face, two feet high, who walked upright and drank a glass of ale. With this anthropoid were on view a hyena, ' a murmo dear, one of the seven sleepers ' and ' the whistler admirable for his extraordinary scent '.

It is a tribute to Mrs Oldfield's power to pull them in, that *The Careless Husband* survived to run those nine consecutive nights.

CHAPTER XI

Blest be the bastard's birth. Through wondrous ways
He shines eccentric like a comet's blaze;
No sickly fruit of faint compliance he,
He stamped in Nature's mint of ecstasy!

R. SAVAGE

Motherhood

IN THE SUMMER of 1705, the love affair between Arthur
Maynwaring and Anne Oldfield ran true to the normal
eighteenth-century form and she presented him with a son,
who was christened Arthur. There had been several ineffectual
attempts by the father's friends, men as well as women, ' some
of them of the highest rank ', to break off the connection,
mainly, it seems, on grounds of Anne's extravagance, which his
modest fortune, they thought, could ill support:

> Engaging Oldfield! who with grace and ease
> Could join the arts to ruin and to please,

wrote her detractor Pope.

If she spent too much of her lover's money on her clothes, it
must be remembered that part of an actress's stock in trade is
to be well dressed:

> The first dramatick rule is have good clothes
> To charm the gay spectator's gentle breast.
> By lace and feather tragedy's expressed
> And heroes die unpitied, if ill-dressed.

Anne's gowns, as the years went by, began to set the fashions at
Court. They were bound with gold lace ' so pure as to come
safely through a fire '. Even Pope was to record:

> The shout, the long exploding note
> At Quin's high plume and Oldfield's petticoat.

A bill for repairing one of these garments has survived: ' For
Mrs Opheilds for niew making a slash'd bodied habit petit-
coate, dressing and binding £2 16s 0d.'

74

At the end of her career, she provided her own jewellery and bought her own stage gowns from an allowance made her by the management. In these latter days, she is heard of going to the theatre, wearing the dress she had put on for dinner at one or other of the great houses. She has been identified with Flavia of the *Tatler*, who:

Was always well dressed; the make of her mind very much contributed to the ornament of her body and her clothes were so exactly fitted that they appeared as it were part of her person. There was such composure in her looks and propriety in her dress that you would think it impossible she should change the garb you one day see her in for anything so becoming, till you next day see her in another.

Two particulars in the portrait of Flavia, however, rule out Anne. Flavia is described as possessing the greatest simplicity of manners, and everyone who sees her is said to know her to be one of quality. A little research proves this paragon to have been, in fact, a Miss Osborne who married Bishop Atterbury.

Anne's humble origin prompted her to extravagance once she had a fashionable lover to foot the bills. In her veins ran the blood of Trooper Oldfield, who galloped so bravely through his patrimony. In her time women's clothes were as expensive as they are to-day. She certainly shared the somewhat Latin view of her lover's friend Joseph Addison:

I consider a woman a beautiful, romantic animal that may be adorned with furs and feathers, pearls and diamonds, ores and silks. The Lynx shall cast its skin at her feet to make her a tippet; the peacock, parrot and swan shall pay contributions to her muff; the sea shall be searched for shells, and the rocks for gems, and every part of nature furnish out its share towards the embellishment of a creature that is the most consummate work of it.

The average eighteenth-century woman may have been a fool, she was at least a well-dressed one.

Clothes apart, Anne was undoubtedly an expensive minx. Horace Walpole, who took breakfast with Mrs Bracegirdle in her old age, tells an anecdote of the Oldfield way of life: ' As Mrs Bracegirdle went out and wanted her clogs, she turned to me, and said, " I remember at the playhouse they used to call:

Mrs Oldfield's chair! Mrs Barry's clogs! and Mrs Bracegirdle's pattens! " [1] Anne's chair, too, was always attended by a couple of footmen.

When Anne was told of her enemies' attempts to end her affair with Maynwaring on grounds of her extravagance, her mother wit and feminine instinct came readily into play. With a brave smile, she whispered in Arthur's ear that ' it was for his honour and interest to break off their alliance '. The result was inevitable. The ingenuous male felt that ' her open frankness only engaged him to her the more firmly ', and he made it very clear to his friends that no attempt to induce him to leave her would succeed. The only result of their onslaught was that from that hour her ' engaging manner more and more entangled him in Cupid's nets '. Arthur's unmarried sister Grisel, who may have led the charge, must have wished she had left well alone.

Maynwaring, although he had no official status, was very close to Marlborough and Godolphin, who headed the government. Their anxieties were to a great extent his. It was, we are told, ' to unbend his mind ' that he delighted in passing his time with a woman ' whose conversation was both soft and pleasant and exactly agreeable to his own '.

The product of a mind thus unbent was christened after his father that summer and proved ' such a rivet to Cupid's chains as bound him much faster to his Venus '. Anne delighted in her little son. She had to look ahead and use her wits to plan for his future. It was no doubt her idea for her lover to talk to Godolphin. The Treasurer expressed himself as being so fond of Maynwaring that he was willing to spend several thousand pounds out of his own pocket in buying out a Mr Donne, Auditor of the Imprests, and conferring the post with its salary of three thousand pounds a year on his friend! This appointment, which solved the problem of young Arthur's future, was the occasion of all sorts of good resolutions. The father ' reduced all his expenses to stated allowances and laid by a considerable part of the income of his auditorship, saying he had been such a fool as to despise money, but now he would do as other men did and endeavour to grow rich '. Unfortunately, a man of thirty-

[1] The patten now supports each frugal dame. – JOHN GAY.

seven does not easily change his habits. ' No man could have a greater contempt for money or more abhorred what was mean or sordid. His company was so much the delight of the great, the gay and the fair. His wines were generally champagne and burgundy ' and their ' corrosive qualities ' began to impair his constitution. Lucky for him that he had Anne's ' care and tender affection '.

★   ★   ★

Was the young Arthur Maynwaring, in fact, Mrs Oldfield's first child? Margaret Saunders, Anne's dresser and very faithful friend, testified that her mistress's only children were Arthur Maynwaring and Charles Churchill, the latter the son of her second established lover after the death of Arthur. ' For was I brought on my oath,' she declared, ' I would swear she had no other; and as to love affairs, I do assure you, I know of none but with the fathers of the gentlemen herein mentioned.' By so saying the lady may be thought to protest too much. Or did she exclude George Farquhar because, at that early date, she did not share Anne's secrets?

But what can be made of the puzzling case of Miss ' Dye ' Bertie, alleged daughter of Mrs Oldfield? Mrs Delaney, at the beginning of her autobiography, mentions that at six years old she was placed under the care of a Mademoiselle Puelle, a refugee (it is gratifying to learn) of a very respectable character. That would be about 1706. This lady undertook not more than twenty scholars at a time, among whom was Lady Jane Douglas[1] (of the celebrated Douglas Cause), and ' Miss Dye Bertie, *a daughter of Mrs Oldfield* who, after leaving school, was the pink of fashion in the beau-monde and married a noble-man '. Who this elegant Diana Bertie was remains a mystery. Even apart from Margaret Saunders's testimony, it does not seem very likely that she was really Anne's daughter. Diana would not go to a boarding school before she was six, which would imply that she was conceived about the years 1699-1700 when Anne was busy with George Farquhar, and when there is no gap in her stage history long enough to allow for childbirth. Who was the father? Dr Doran, the nineteenth-century

[1] For her story the present author's *Chancellor Thurlow* (pp. 47, 48) may be consulted.

authority on the English stage, inserted a query about the elusive Miss Diana in the Press and received no reply. He left a manuscript note to the effect that, far from wedding a noble-man, she married a Mr J. Cator. As far as dates go, her father might well be Peregrine Bertie, who was born in 1686 and created Duke of Ancaster in 1715, to die in 1742. Vice-Chamberlain and Privy Councillor, he is described as a fine gentleman, who had both wit and learning (though ' I never observed a grain of either ' commented Dean Swift sourly), and as such might well have frequented the Greenroom at Drury Lane. But there is no record that he was one of Mrs Oldfield's admirers. Again, there is Montague Bertie, second Earl of Abingdon, who was born about 1673 and died in 1743. His second wife was the widow of General Charles Churchill, brother of the Duke of Marlborough and father of Brigadier Charles Churchill, Mrs Oldfield's next established lover. Is it here possible dimly to conceive how some confusion might have arisen in Mrs Delany's memory? There the mystery must be allowed to rest, with the grave doubt that Anne Oldfield ever had a daughter ' Dye '.[1]

*   *   *

Whatever else happened to her, Mrs Oldfield's career on the stage had to go on. The new plays in which she acted that season were, in the main, neither distinguished nor successful. *The Basset Table* by Mrs Centlivre, in which Anne played the part of Lady Reveller, who kept the basset table, was a failure. Cibber's seasonal offering was a classical tragedy in verse called *Perolla and Izadora* with a plot taken from the twenty-third book of Livy. In its prologue he adjures his audience not:

> To think in plays that language is the whole;
> Style is but the body, fable is the soul.

Even had Livy or Cibber produced a good plot, the verse is so flat that the play is unreadable and, if Anne could make nothing of it, presumably unactable.

Steele's *Tender Husband*, based on Molière's *Les Précieuses*

---

[1] It is no doubt a meaningless coincidence that in a letter written from Rome on 8 January 1738, S. Crisp tells his grandmother ' our most particular intimates are . . . young Churchill, the general's son by Mrs Oldfield, and Bertie and his governor '. *Notes and Queries* 24 Dec: 1948.

Ridicules, produced in April 1705, was a different sort of failure. Anne played Biddy Tipkin, a banker's niece with a dowry of ten thousand pounds plus five thousand pounds' worth of her mother's jewellery. Her impassioned reading of romances has so rarefied her mind that she longs for a name ' that glides through half a dozen tender syllables ' like Elismonde or Deidamia. The part gives every sign of having been written with an eye on Mrs Oldfield. Her accents can be heard when Biddy expostulates with her aunt: ' Do you think I can ever marry a man that's true and hearty? What a peasant-like amour do these coarse words impart;' or when she declares: ' It looks so *ordinary* to go out at a door to be married. Indeed I ought to be taken out of a window and run away with! ' Her head is full of shepherds, knights, groves and streams, and her suitor, played by Wilks, is driven to profess that he has been himself a great traveller in fairyland. Notwithstanding a highly unedifying sub-plot, Steele protested as usual that he had been careful to avoid anything that might look ' ill-natured, immoral or prejudicial to what the better part of mankind hold sacred and honourable '. In spite of so much sweetness and light, and even stranger, in spite of Anne's brilliant performance as Biddy, the play failed at its original production. April was late in the season for a new play, and on the fourth night (it only ran five) there was only £26 11*s* o*d* in the house. The author's contract called for a gross of not less than forty pounds on that night if the play was to be kept on, and off it came, with proceedings in Chancery to follow at the instance of that ready litigant Dick Steele.

Biddy was to become one of Anne's favourite parts and she appeared in many successful revivals. Plays might come, and plays might go, but Anne's career went on. It is a professional actress's mission to be undeterred by failure. She had not the temperament that goes sour on a playwright who has provided her with a ' flop ', though the author must always expect to shoulder the blame. It is the business of the management to explore and risk the pains of failure, as bravely as it reaps the rewards of success. Anne knew this and the day was coming when Steele was to provide her with one of the triumphs of her life.

CHAPTER XII

There is no scandal like rags nor any crime so shameful as poverty.

G. FARQUHAR

Re-enter the Captain

A DANGEROUS rival to the legitimate theatre had come to maturity. Italian opera, with its tenor *castrati*, was exciting the scorn, and the apprehension, of the patrons of regular drama. ' People accustomed to opera ', said Dennis, ' are as ill-prepared to judge of a good tragedy as children that are eating sugar plums are to taste champagne or burgundy.' Again: ' A musical voice is natural to some species of birds but always accidental to men; for which reason a cock nightingale sings better than Nicolini without being taught – or without being gelt for the matter.'

It must have shocked Mrs Oldfield to find her lover an amateur of this new form of art. Fond of music and no mean performer on the spinet, Maynwaring gave in, says his biographer, to the Polite Taste. His fellow members of the Kit-cat Club were heavy subscribers to the new house in the Haymarket which soon became exclusively associated with opera. True, Arthur Maynwaring did not desert his allegiance to Drury Lane, and when the opera *Camilla* was presented there in opposition to the Italian offerings at the Haymarket, he contributed a prologue. Promptly forgiving his dereliction, Anne spoke it beautifully.

Arthur was taking to politics, too, seriously, and standing for Preston, where he was in due course elected. Though attendance in the House was not, in Queen Anne's day, an exacting affair, Anne could not but wish that his manifold interests did not take so much of his time. Still she knew that her lover was not the sort to be ridden on a tight rein. It was with a sigh that she turned to meet the smile of George Farquhar, who stood once more ready to re-enter her life.

But now their relationship was changed. It was the pleasant one of leading lady and author. Even had Anne not been deeply in love with Arthur and a one-man woman (or more strictly a one-man-at-a-time woman), her firm principle of having nothing to do with married men forbade any re-awakening of sentiment. For George was married. An heiress, he had told his friends boastfully, a widow with two daughters and seven hundred pounds a year for him to spend. Alas! the playwright had fallen into a trap, that might have had its inspiration in one of his own comedies. The fortune was mythical, only the two daughters were real. George's pockets were emptier than ever.

He turned over and over in his brain an idea he had for a new play, based on his own experiences in the army – for Captain Farquhar's commission had materialized and was now a practical reality. In the course of his military duties in Shropshire, he had met a wonderful girl, a Miss Beverly, daughter of the Recorder of Shrewsbury. What a play he could write round her and, if he could persuade his lost Penelope to play her, what cheerful music the coins would chink in his pocket!

What a piece of luck, too, that Penelope had developed into a rising star! He had always known she would. Since Mrs Verbruggen's death, he had often watched her play the lead admirably in revivals of his two old comedies *The Constant Couple* and its less successful sequel *Sir Harry Wildair*. . . . Mrs Rogers and Mrs Oldfield, he remembered, had nearly come to blows over who should play Lady Lurewell. True, the Beverly character was rather off Penelope's usual beat. He would have to exercise all his charm. . . .

*   *   *

Sylvia was a fresh conception that brought new life to the stereotyped characters that litter the moribund comedies of the day. Listen to the stock fine lady that Anne was always playing describe her life to an admirer:

I lie in bed till noon, dress all afternoon, dine in the evening and play cards till midnight – What do you talk of? – New fashions and new plays – How often do you go to church? – Twice a year or oftener, according as my husband gives me new clothes! – Pray madam, what books do you read? – I read lewd plays and winning

F

romances – Who is it you love? – My page, my monkey and my lap dog.

Sylvia was new. In fitting the part to Anne, Farquhar was anticipating Di Vernon and was harking back to the girl he knew before Cibber's tawdry pen had typed her into a Lady Betty Modish, before Arthur Maynwaring's admiration had formed her into the mould of the toasts of the Kit-cat.

Hear Sylvia describe herself:

So far as to be troubled with neither spleen, colic nor vapours, I need no salt for my stomach, no hartshorn for my head nor wash for my complexion. I can gallop all morning after the hunting horn and all evening after a fiddle. In short I can do everything with my father, but drink and shoot flying.

Needless to say, in *The Recruiting Officer* Sylvia disguises herself as a man (Anne still liked playing in breeches) and offers to take the Queen's shilling in order to be near the man of her heart, Captain Plume, played of course by Wilks. Nevertheless, the play has a refreshing flavour of reality and is full of well-observed, good acting parts. In the epilogue Farquhar could not resist a dig at his supplanter in Penelope's heart, with his appreciation for the opera *Camilla* and its composer Marc Antonio Buononcini. Drum and fife, writes Captain Farquhar, play the Grenadier March, recently performed with wonderful success at the operas of Vigo and Blenheim to the applause of all Europe – except of the French, who found it a little too rough. 'Ladies, we must own that this music of ours is not altogether as soft as Buononcini's. Yet we dare affirm that it has laid more people asleep than all the Camillas in the world.' Farquhar felt he had scored over Sir Arthur Maynwaring.

The Recruiting Officer was well received and did what Farquhar had hoped. It provided its author with three benefit nights. If Mrs Oldfield's art was sufficient to improve the fortunes of an old lover, she also did not lack a business sense that benefited herself. On 15 August 1706 she went to the Lord Chamberlain's Office and signed an advantageous contract to join Vanbrugh's company at the Queen's Theatre, Haymarket, which was about to abandon its exclusive opera policy.

Her brief contract was headed:

Agreement between John Vanbrugh Esq. and Mrs Ann Oldfield for acting in her Majesty's Company of comedians in the Haymarket, August the 15th 1706.

It runs:

That for every day a play shall be acted by the company under his direction or any person deputed by him, she shall receive the sum of thirteen shillings and four pence.

That she shall have a benefit play paying forty pounds constant charge with the incidents, she submitting herself to the rules, orders and settled forfeitures of the House.

This being signed by the parties and lodged in my Lord Chamberlain's office with his Lordship's approbation.

The contract is signed ' J. Vanbrugh ' and 'Ann Oldfield ', spelt on this occasion without an ' e '. Her silver tones did not yet command top prices. A few years later Anastasia Robinson, fated to end as bride to the erratic Lord Peterborough, received for the season's singing at the opera five hundred pounds and a benefit, plus a gold watch if a profit was shown. Mrs Oldfield's four pounds a week was at least an improvement on her Drury Lane salary, which had been fixed at fifty shillings ever since March 1703.

★   ★   ★

The Queen's Theatre, Haymarket, had been built, regardless of acoustics, under the direction of Vanbrugh and Congreve. There, Anne Oldfield found Betterton, Barry and Bracegirdle, who had moved from the theatre in Lincoln's Inn Fields. Besides Robert Wilks, other actors and actresses, including Estcourt, Norris and Jane Rogers, accompanied Anne in the exodus from Drury Lane. The company was a very strong one and competition for popular favour intense. The combination of forces with the three B's had a decisive influence on the development of Anne's technique. Not only had she the force of example and the spur of competition, but the addition of their repertory of plays added to her scope. The variety of her powers could not be known until she was seen in a variety of characters. Thus in the season 1706-7 she appeared in Ben Jonson's two great plays *Volpone*, where she played Celia, and *The Silent Woman*, in which she took the name part against

Betterton's Morose. In Dryden's *Spanish Friar*, when Mrs Barry played Leonora, she took Elvira. In Southerne's *Oroonoko* she played Imoinda, in Otway's *Orphan* Monimia, in Etherege's *Comical Revenge* the Widow Rich. In addition she acted the parts she had created in Steele's *Tender Husband*, Cibber's *Careless Husband*, Farquhar's recent success *The Recruiting Officer*, with the parts she had inherited in Crowne's *Sir Courtly Nice* and in Fletcher's *Pilgrim*.

Then there were new plays. Mrs Centlivre made her regular contribution and so did Colley Cibber. Great hopes were based on *The Platonick Lady* by the prolific authoress. A prologue was furnished by Farquhar, once more the playwright of the moment, and the play was very strongly cast. Betterton, Wilks, Booth and Cibber all featured, while Mrs Bracegirdle played Lucinda and Mrs Oldfield Isabella (who dresses up as a farmer's daughter and passes herself off on her noble lover as one of his tenants). In spite of this spate of talent, the play opened on a Monday and closed for ever on the following Thursday.

Cibber's inventive powers were momentarily at a low ebb and he had combined two pieces by Dryden into a ' new ' play *The Comical Lovers*, in which Anne had the part of Florimel created by Nell Gwynne at the original Dryden version. Other parts were played by Mrs Bracegirdle, Mrs Porter, Wilks, Booth and Cibber himself. His concoction had more luck than Mrs Centlivre's effort and was frequently revived.

But the new plays which created the greatest excitement in this distinguished season were Farquhar's last comedy *The Beaux Stratagem* (revived as recently as 1949 by John Clements for a long run at the Phœnix Theatre) and Edmund Smith's forgotten adaptation of Racine's tragedy, which he called *Phædra and Hippolitus*.

Edmund Smith was a Master of Arts, ' an Oxford man extremely read in Greek ', who had been sent down from the House for writing a lampoon on the Dean. He was nicknamed Captain Rag from the slovenly way he dressed. Like some Third Programme figure of to-day he seems to have hypnotized the intelligentsia. ' It must not be forgotten how jealously Mr Addison espoused his interest with all the elegant judgment

and diffusive good-nature for which that accomplished gentleman was so justly valued by mankind.' For Smith's unactable
adaptation, his first and last venture on the stage, Addison
contributed a prologue and Prior an epilogue. Lesser men were
taken in too. Phædra, Egerton declared, made a finer figure
under Mr Smith's handling than she had either at Rome or
Athens. It surpassed the French version, preserving all Racine's
regular beauty and moving softness.

Impressed by Addison's support, the Haymarket management cast the play superbly, with Betterton as Theseus, the
newly arrived Booth as Hippolytus, Mrs Barry as Phædra and
Mrs Oldfield as Ismena. ' Who could sit unmoved at a recital
of the passions of Theseus' Queen or the Princess Ismena, when
a Barry and an Oldfield were the pleaders? ' Anne saw through
the pretensions of the play at once. She and the author were at
loggerheads during rehearsal. Usually the easiest actress in the
world to handle, (' she was tractable ', says Cibber, who regularly produced her, ' and less presuming in her station than
several that had not half her pretensions to be troublesome',)
both the imperfections of the play and the self-assurance of its
author upset her.

Mrs Barry got on with him better. When she objected to her
exit at the end of Act IV, Smith took several turns of the stage
and, after a moment's thought, produced six lines of flowing
(and no doubt, banal) verse that got her off to her complete
satisfaction.

The first night came. All began well with Addison's prologue,
spoken by Robert Wilks, complaining of the vogue of operatic
tenors who:

> In songs and airs express their martial fire,
> Combat in trills and in a Fuge expire.
> While lulled by sound and undisturbed by wit,
> Calm and serene you indolently sit,
> And from the dull fatigue of thinking free,
> Hear the facetious fiddles' repartee:
> Our homespun authors must forsake the field
> And Shakespeare to the soft Scarlatti yield.

But the play itself would not do. The audience knew better
than the men of letters. In vain Mrs Oldfield and Mrs Barry

exerted all their tragic power. The character of Ismena, said the critics, showed Anne in a light of perfection ' hardly to be expressed '. Who was not pierced to the heart as she pronounced the lines:

> Now if I live 'tis only for Hippolytus
> And with an equal joy I'll die to save him.
> Yes, for his sake I'll go a willing shade
> And wait his coming in the Elysian fields
> And there enquire of each descending ghost
> Of my loved hero's welfare, life and honour. . . .

She dismissed the audience, comparatively happy, with Matthew Prior's epilogue, but the epitaph of the play's four-night run was written by the *Spectator*: ' Would one think it possible, at a time when an author lived that was able to write *Phædra and Hippolitus*, for a people to be so stupidly fond of the Italian Opera as scarce to give a third day's hearing to that admirable tragedy? ' Addison went on to reveal that a friend had advised Smith to turn his play into an opera libretto. The advice may well have been good.

★ ★ ★

At the age of twenty-nine George Farquhar lay dying in squalor; dying of the tuberculosis he had invited in the cellar he described to Penelope; dying of dissipation and poverty. Prophetically he had written of Comedy: ' Naked she came into the world and it is to be feared, like her professors, will go naked out.' Ever optimistic, his friend Robert Wilks lent him twenty guineas and urged him to start a new play. *The Beaux Stratagem*, the best-constructed, best-characterized, wittiest, gayest product of his pen was the gallant result.

During rehearsals of the play, Wilks tactfully conveyed to the dying dramatist an objection that Anne had made to her part. Like all actors and actresses, she was struggling against anything that might in her opinion make the character she was playing unsympathetic to the audience. This time she wanted Mrs Sullen formally divorced, before she was handed over by her sottish husband to Wilks.

' Tell her ', smiled Farquhar, ' that I will, if she pleases, solve that immediately by getting a real divorce, marrying her myself and giving her my bond that she shall be a widow in less than a fortnight.'

Farquhar always put himself into his plays. His preoccupation with the problem of incompatibility between husband and wife and its solution by Milton's doctrine of divorce by mutual consent, stems from his own married life, which was a financial and emotional fiasco:

Mrs Sullen	In the first place I can't drink ale with you.
Sullen	Nor can I drink tea with you.
Mrs Sullen	I can't hunt with you.
Sullen	Nor can I dance with you.
Mrs Sullen	I hate cocking and racing.
Sullen	I abhor ombre and picquet. . . . What singing was that I heard just now?
Mrs Sullen	The singing in your head, my dear; you complained of it all day.
Sullen	You're impertinent.
Mrs Sullen	I have been so since I became one flesh with you.
Sullen	One flesh! Rather two carcases joined unnaturally together.
Mrs Sullen	Or rather a living soul coupled to a dead body.

Poor Farquhar paid dearly for his heiress – a pity for his sake he never made up his mind to employ the parson of St Ann's to bind him to his Penelope!

* * *

It is always easy to detect imaginary likenesses, but may not the barmaid Cherry give Farquhar's picture of the girl he found at the *Mitre*? ' The baggage has a pert *je ne sais quoi*, she reads plays, keeps a monkey . . .' While Mrs Sullen depicts her as he saw her when life and the stage had formed her young womanhood? ' Country pleasures! racks and torments! Dost think that my limbs were made for leaping of ditches and clambering over stiles? '

He lived to see his play produced. It was an immediate success, though cuts had to be made after the first night. It is a tribute to Mrs Oldfield's adaptability, or to the strength of mind of the producer, that the whole of one of her scenes, the episode with the French prisoner, was cut. A brief compliment was paid her in the author's preface to the published version. The representation of the play, Farquhar commented, ' cannot be matched '. Those were the last words he wrote. He died on the eleventh night of the run, which provided him an extra benefit. Four days later he was buried at Robert Wilks's expense at St Martin-in-the-Fields. The actor found a note addressed to him among his dead friend's papers:

Dear Bob, I have not anything to leave thee to perpetuate my memory but two helpless girls. . . .

*   *   *

Meanwhile the management was finding the Haymarket company too brightly star-studded. The more mature Mrs Bracegirdle and Mrs Oldfield in the full flush of her youth (she was now twenty-four) were competing for the same parts in comedy. With characteristic hard-heartedness the management preferred the newcomer: ' Mrs Oldfield's voice, figure and manner of playing made her shine out the brightest star.' They gave unmistakable sign of their preference by putting Anne's benefit ahead of Mrs Bracegirdle's. This deeply offended the elder actress. There is a story, apparently apocryphal (for no record exists of any such successive performances), that the two actresses agreed that a test should be made of their powers. Betterton's comedy *The Amorous Widow* was chosen to be performed two nights running with the part of Mrs Brittle played the first time by Mrs Bracegirdle and the second by Mrs Oldfield. The audience was to be umpire. And with such loud applause on the second night did it fulfil its function that Mrs Bracegirdle left the stage for good. However little truth there may be in this story, it is a fact that Mrs Bracegirdle quitted the stage after one season of competition with Anne, to outlive in retirement her rival by many years.

Another story is told of Anne's acting in the same play. The part of Mrs Brittle's betrayed husband, Barnaby Brittle, was normally played by Dicky Norris, that inspired cuckold. One day Dicky was ill and Cibber understudied. A conversation that took place between Colley and Anne reveals a robust attitude towards sex:

Tell me, Nanny, how do you like your new husband? – Why very well; but not half so well as Dicky! – How so? – Why, you are too important a figure! Norris has so diminutive a figure and so sneaking a look, he seems formed on purpose for horns and I always make him a cuckold with a hearty good will.

On the last night of this eventful season His Excellency the Russian Ambassador came to see Mrs Oldfield play in Carlisle's old play *The Fortune Hunters*. She may have been less flattered by that attention than might be expected, for the envoy was not a very satisfactory character. He had run up bills wholesale: £119 2s 6d for boxes at the theatre and the opera, which the Lord Chamberlain had to pay; £26 9s 0d for damage done at his lodgings, and so on. The day he was leaving for Russia, his coach was stopped in the Haymarket and his person detained for a debt of three hundred and sixty pounds. He paid the bill but protested to the Queen at the insult.

CHAPTER XIII

Sometime let Gorgeous Tragedy
In sceptred pall come sweeping by.
MILTON

Tragedy Queen

THIS YEAR ANNE, with her wonted generosity, came to the rescue of one of her most savage critics. She had not forgotten how Charles Gildon (trained a Roman Catholic priest, but converted to free thought and ending a deist) had lashed her in her early days as rubbish that ought to be swept off the stage with the dust and filth. Already, as an unsuccessful playwright, he had been in trouble with a not very exacting censorship, and now in 1707 he came in conflict with the law, as a journalist. In a couple of pamphlets drearily enough entitled ' A letter from the Princess Sophia to His Grace the Archbishop of Canterbury ' and ' Another from Hanover written by Sir Rowland Gascoigne ', he ventured on the slippery ground of the succession to the throne of England. A warrant was issued for his arrest and imprisonment in Newgate followed. He was allowed bail but stood his trial in February and was found guilty. The dreaded punishment of the pillory loomed before his eyes.

In this emergency the offender wondered what assistance he could summon. His best hope lay in any pull he possessed in stage circles. There was Sir Richard Steele, who had Court connections, and, if he could enlist his help, Sir Arthur Maynwaring, who had the *entrée* everywhere. If Sir Arthur's mistress would only forgive those unfortunate strictures, perhaps she could be induced to put in a word for her critic. Anne's memory was short and her compassion great. She brought the hapless writer's case to her lover, who promised to further a petition to the Sovereign, if Steele would pen it.

To H.M. Queen Anne on behalf of Charles Gildon [memorialized the playwright]: That your petitioner has, by an unhappy mistake, and not by malicious design against the happiness and quiet of Your Majesty's Government, been concerned in publishing a pam-

phlet called Sir R. Gascoigne's letter etc. That your petitioner has
had a liberal education and fortune, and expects this term a sentence
worse than death for the same. That he is under the greatest sorrow
and contrition for this his high offence. . . .

Harley, the Secretary now, received this petition, backed by
a note from Maynwaring. He had the penalty fixed at a
merciful hundred-pound fine, which, since Gildon did not
possess that sum, he later waived, again at Maynwaring's
request. Truly, the ' rubbish of the stage ' proved its use.

*   *   *

By now another, more considerable, playwright whose work
has been unfairly forgotten was moving into Anne's orbit. This
was Nicholas Rowe, whose play about Hengist and Horsa *The
Royal Convert* starred Anne and Mrs Barry at the end of the
year 1707.

Rowe was a long-nosed, double-chinned man of thirty-one
who could laugh all day, graceful but masculine, vain of his
looks but untidy. He was the son of a barrister of good Devonshire family. After a brief experience of Westminster School,
Nicholas was himself called to the Bar at the Middle Temple.
Then his father died and his inheritance enabled him to continue to live in the Temple and devote his life to writing plays
in bland, blank verse. His first tragedy to see the light was *The
Ambitious Step-Mother*, an Oriental palace intrigue with a good
plot full of treachery, suicide, attempted rape, revenge and
ultimate punishment of the guilty. The psychological formula
he followed was indicated in his preface:

The audience should be struck with terror in several parts, but
always go away with pity, a sort of regret proceeding from good
nature, which, though an uneasiness, is not altogether disagreeable
to the person that feels it.

Betterton produced his play at Lincoln's Inn Fields and Rowe
took the opportunity to fall in love with the unapproachable
Mrs Bracegirdle. The tragedy was generously praised by his
rival for the lady's favours and fellow-barrister of the Middle
Temple, William Congreve. Many of its lines bear quotation,
such as the description of the neurotic Cleone:

. . . . A melancholy girl.
Such in her infancy her temper was,
Soft even beyond her sex's tenderness;
By nature pitiful and apt to grieve
For the mishaps of others and to make
The sorrows of the wretched world her own. . . .
She seeks some shady solitary grove
Or by the gentle murmurs of some brook
Sits sadly listening to some tale of sorrow
Till with her tears she swell the narrow stream.

This success was followed by Rowe's favourite play, *Tamerlane*, which also featured the Betterton-Barry-Bracegirdle trio. Like his author, Tamerlane is found to be an earnest Whig, the reverse of Marlowe's more full-blooded conception. He was a convinced pacifist: ' Oh, thou fell monster War! '; an early adherent to the ideals of the United Nations:

. . . . Well was it for the world
When on their borders neighbouring Princes met,
Frequent in friendly parle, by cool debates
Preventing wasteful war.

and a confirmed respecter of liberty of conscience. Tamerlane stood in fact for an idealized, if priggish, William III and the villain Bajazet for a despicable Louis XIV. It was not until the incessant provocation of Bajazet's ignoble plots causes him finally to lose his temper, that Tamerlane sentences his opponent:

Closed in a cage like some destructive beast,
I'll have thee borne about in public view
A great example of the righteous vengeance
That waits on cruelty.

This demure melodrama was performed annually on 4 November, anniversary of William's landing, until well into the nineteenth century. The occasion often engendered political warmth: as when in Dublin in 1712 the players refused to speak Doctor Garth's prologue, commemorating the Revolution. Whereat Mr Dudley Moore, ' a gentleman of good family and standing, stepped on the stage and read the prologue with general applause and good liking. Two or three obscure persons hissed but they were drowned by the loud claps of the numbers of honest gentlemen, well-affected to the memory of their great deliverer '.

Of *The Fair Penitent*, Rowe's next offering, which later became one of Anne Oldfield's greatest rôles, Doctor Johnson wrote: ' There is scarcely any work of any poet at once so interesting by the fable and so delightful in the language.' An excursion into farce with *The Biter* amused nobody but its author, who was seen at the first night, rocking with laughter at his own jokes. These depended mainly, like too many of W. S. Gilbert's, on the humour of growing old. The title depends on the craze of the moment for ' biting '. (A condemned felon sells his body to a surgeon. As he pockets the payment, ' Bit! ', he exclaims, ' I am to be hanged in chains! ')

Rowe reverted to melodrama with *Ulysses*, still for the three B's, now acting at the Queen's Theatre in the Haymarket. It ran nine nights and was honoured with new costumes and sets. The prologue drew a topical parallel between the Trojan War and Marlborough's campaigns:

> We have our chaste Penelopes who mourn
> Their widowed beds and wait their lords' return.
> We have our heroes too who bravely bear
> Far from their homes the dangers of the war.

The reign of Mrs Bracegirdle and Mrs Barry had now come to an end and Rowe transferred his allegiance to their great successor, Mrs Oldfield, who combined in her single art the light comedy of the one with the deep-bosomed tragedy of the other. After the less remarkable melodrama of *The Royal Convert*, he was to write for Anne his great ' she-tragedies ' *Jane Shore* and *Lady Jane Grey*, by far the most successful serious plays of the period. Anne liked saying that ' all the merit she acquired in the modulation of her tones was from Rowe reading his own tragedies to her ', but this may be discounted as one of the normal insincerities of the dressing-room. It is enough that their interaction on each other's art was entirely happy. Rowe was an early student and admirer of Shakespeare, writing his *Jane Shore* in imitation of his style, though Pope unkindly, and inaccurately, said that the only resemblance was in the single borrowed line 'And so good-morrow to ye, good master lieutenant! '. He was the first editor of the Bard, utilizing his friendship with Betterton to include the actor's gleanings of Stratford tradition. For his elaborate edition he was only paid the sum of thirty-five guineas, but money was little object to him. Beside his private income and benefits from his numerous stage successes, he held sinecures to the value of twelve hundred pounds a year. For the last three years of his life, he was Poet Laureate, grinding out dismal odes in praise of the uninspiring Hanoverian monarchs:

> See thy George for this is he;
> On his right hand waiting free
> Britain and fair liberty.
> Every good is in his face,
> Every open honest grace,
> Thou great Plantagenet! Immortal be thy race!

In *The Royal Convert* Anne was an Ancient British lady, a Christian, with two Saxon princes in love with her. One of them, played by Wilks, marries her secretly and when betrothal to a Saxon princess, played by Mrs Barry, is forced on him by King Hengist, he attempts to kill himself. A later act depicts a ' temple adorned according to the superstition of the ancient Saxons, in the middle are placed their three principal idols Thor, Woden and Freya '. Wilks shows great nobility of soul, refusing all Mrs Barry's offers and remaining true to his Christian bride. ' The scene draws and discovers the inner part of the temple. A fire is prepared on one of the altars, near it are placed a rack, knives, axes and other instruments of torture, several priests attending as for a sacrifice.' Mrs Oldfield, refusing to deny her faith, is placed on the rack to Mrs Barry's infinite satisfaction. But all ends happily with Hengist's opportune death, after an abortive attempt on Mrs Oldfield's virtue and a prophetic vision of the Act of Union of 1707:

> Of royal race a British Queen shall rise
> Great, gracious, pious, fortunate and wise,
> Auspicious Heaven on all her days shall shine
> And with eternal UNION bless her British Isles.

In spite of what seem to-day manifold absurdities, the plot is well-constructed and much of the verse more than adequate:

Wilks   Courts may boast of Beauty,
But Love is seldom found to dwell among them.
Mrs Barry Then Courts are wretched.
Wilks   So they seem to Love;
From pride, from wealth, from business and from power,
Loathing he flies and seeks the peaceful village.
He seeks the cottage in the tufted grove,
The clear cool brook and the deep woody glade,
Bright winter fires and summer evenings' suns.
These he prefers to gilded roofs and crowns.
Here he delights to pair the constant swain
With the sweet, unaffected, yielding maid.
Here is his empire. . . .

The part of Hengist, designed for Betterton, was played by a young man, Barton Booth. Booth was a comparative newcomer who had quickly leapt into the front rank of tragedians. Five feet eight inches tall, his body was graceful and athletic. Though he spoke blank verse in the solemn, articulate manner of the day, his voice was quiet and harmonious, with all the inflexions, it was said, from flute to trumpet. ' Well-mouthed ' Booth was Pope's epithet. He was indolent or temperamental and did not always give his best, unlike Wilks, whose diligence was so indefatigable that he seemed to love it, like virtue, for its own sake. Booth had no sense of humour and carried ' his reverence for the buskin ' so far that he would not allow a smile in any part of a tragic rôle. This may explain his lack of enthusiasm, unique among his contemporaries, for Mrs Oldfield's tragedy and for Wilks's acting as a whole. Anne, a born comedienne, would eagerly seize on every light and shade in a tragic part. Indeed, it was not until this season and a resounding success in a revival of Nat Lee's *Mithridates* that she became quite reconciled to play full-blown tragedy.

Tragic acting in the first half of the eighteenth century was not considered effective without a great show of vocal pyrotechnics and exaggerated gesture. Diction was either given a musical cadence, if French models were favoured, or a monotonous rhythm, when native methods were preferred. James Quin, a younger contemporary of Anne's, used to produce ' a

deep full tone, accompanied by a sawing gesture which had
more of the senate than the stage. He rolled out his heroics with
an air of dignified indifference '. Turgid vociferation and an
effeminate whine were mistaken respectively for a display of
the heroic and the tender passion. The actor exploited his own
personality and did not seek to explore the psychology or
character of the part he was playing. Fifty years later the
Reverend Thomas Newton could write to Garrick, ' What
strikes me is the variety of your acting and your being so totally
different a man in *Lear* from what you are in *Richard*. There is a
sameness in every other actor.' It was not until the maturity of
Charles Macklin that the tradition began to be broken. ' I
spoke so familiar ', he declared, ' and so little in the hoity-toity
tone of tragedy of that day.'

Criticism was levelled at the slackness of actors on the stage
when not immediately involved in the action. They were to be
seen whispering to each other or bowing to friends in the Pit.
Doctor Johnson said of a popular favourite of his day that she
had no more thought of the play than a shoemaker has of the
piece of leather out of which he is cutting a boot. Wilks was a
notable exception. He never relaxed and always gave of his
best. But his best was not tragedy; his epoch criticized his jerky,
uneven delivery in heroic rôles: it possibly seemed over-
realistic.

The fault of monotony was less evident with actresses, who
had only recently supplanted boy actors and had not had time
to succumb to the weight of tradition. Anne, with her comedy
training and instinct, was a natural rebel. Her quick observa-
tion made it inevitable for her to characterize each part she was
playing. Her tragic technique might appear to the present-day
theatre-goer over-emphatic. To compete with the large number
of parts she had to be ready to render, her attitudes and gestures
had been stylized. ' The chief indication of the mind ', says
Steele, ' is in the gesture, or indeed in the case of sorrow, no
gesture.' If the nouns dignity and majesty occur too frequently
for our more half-hearted taste in appreciations of Anne's
playing of tragedy, the stilted and unrealistic nature of the
material she had to work in must be remembered. Tragedy,
says Cibber, thinking no doubt of his own plays, is too often

written in lofty disregard of nature. The silver accents of her voice overcame much of the handicap of the verse she had to render and redeemed it from the fashionable monotony: ' Her voice was sweet, strong, piercing and melodious; her pronunciation voluble, distinct and musical, and her emphasis always placed where the spirit of the sense in her periods only demanded it.' In fact, unlike many actors to-day, she understood what she was saying.

Her fine eyes she used to great purpose. She is said to have told her audience as much with them as with her words. Conditions of lighting and proximity of actress to audience make this less incredible that it would be to-day.

If the outmoded virtue of dignity was the hallmark of her tragic acting, the completely discredited attribute of gentility qualifies her comedy.

Why [asked Horace Walpole] are there so few genteel comedies, but because most comedies are written by men not of that sphere? Etherege, Congreve, Vanbrugh, and Cibber wrote genteel comedy because they lived in the best company and Mrs Oldfield played it so well, because she not only followed but often set the fashion.

What now seems snobbery pervades the century. What that century called genteel was nothing worse than possessing an acute sense of style, without which there can be no first-class acting. Anne's bearing was compared very favourably with Garrick's. Theophilus Cibber imagines Dapper Dan, as he calls him, just joining the immortals, and watches:

> Wilks leading Oldfield through the crowd;
> Her elegance of visage, form and mien,
> With majesty and smiling grace commixt,
> Claimed from the sensible, respectful love.

Garrick offers to join them, but Oldfield smiles and tells him: ' She chose for her companions the elegant, the polite and such whose manner was expression of spirited delicacy and genteel deportment.'

Her comic range was great. In the season of her triumph in the tragedy of *Mithridates* she played lead in a very varied list of comedy revivals. The best known to-day is Congreve's *Love*

G

for Love, in which she played Angelica. But Beaumont and
Fletcher's *Rule a Wife*, Dryden's *Spanish Friar*, Mrs Behn's
bawdy masterpiece *The Rover*, Steele's *Funeral*, and Shadwell's
Squire of Alsatia, in which she appeared for the benefit of her
friend Susan Verbruggen's orphan daughter, all bore witness
to Anne Oldfield's comic versatility.

The only two new comedies came both from the fertile pen
of Colley Cibber. In *The Double Gallant* the playwright, after
his wont, had plundered Thomas Corneille and Charles
Burnaby. Lady Dainty, Burnaby's heroine, says to her maid:
' Peace, good impertinence, I tell thee no woman of quality is,
or should be, in perfect health.' In Cibber's version Mrs Dainty,
played by Anne, assures her audience that ' the apoplexy, the
gout and the vapours are all peculiar to the nobility ', and the
whole part is built on Burnaby's character. For once the theft
was punished. Some spy in the pay of the rival management
gave away the plagiarist's plans, and the night before *The
Double Gallant* was put on at the Haymarket, Burnaby's
Reform'd Wife was maliciously revived at Drury Lane. In vain
Mrs Oldfield babbled of her collection of ailments; in vain Mrs
Rogers played her familiar rôle of the prude; in vain Mrs Cross
exercised her sex appeal as the rakish teenager. In spite even
of Colley's disarming prologue:

> Could those who never tried, conceive the sweat,
> The toil required to make a play complete,
> They'd pardon or encourage all that would
> Pretend to be but tolerably good!
> Plot, wit and humour's hard to meet in one,
> And yet without 'em all, all's lamely done. . . .
> Nay, even altered plays like old houses mended,
> Cost little less than new, before they're ended

the play proved for the time being a failure, although in the
next thirty years it scored an imposing list of revivals.

Cibber's other new play, *The Lady's Last Stake*, had an even
stronger cast. Mrs Oldfield had the star part as Mrs Conquest,
who, unrecognized in male attire, is escorted by her unwitting
admirer behind the scenes at the theatre, where ' there are
ladies of all sorts, coquettes, prudes and virgins (they say) '.
Mrs Rogers was once again the indomitable prude and Mrs

Cross the not less unavoidable teenager. Then there was Mrs Barry, Wilks, and Cibber himself. After a bad start, the play picked up and was rated by its author in the same class of hit as his *Careless Husband,* that vehicle of Anne's first London triumph. The plot was this time Cibber's own, even, it might be said, doubly so; for it was the plot of *The Careless Husband* in reverse. Mrs Barry's maid, who has seen that play, describes the scene drawn from the family life of the Bretts, to her mistress:

A lady comes in and catches her husband fast asleep with her own woman and then goes softly to him – And strangles him in his sleep? – No, madam! – She strangles the woman? – No, madam. She only lays her handkerchief gently over his head for fear he should catch cold – Horrid! And what becomes of the poor-spirited creature? – When the gentleman wakes, he grows so ashamed of his wickedness and sensible of her virtue that he afterwards proves the best husband in the world.

But Mrs Barry, in the part of Lady Wronglove, is made of sterner stuff, and in comparable circumstances heads firmly for divorce.

This was the last new play Elizabeth Barry was to grace. The season saw her retirement from the stage, to which she was only to return with Anne Bracegirdle for the single night of Betterton's last benefit. On that occasion Steele mentions that the stage was covered with spectators of both sexes, and ' when the curtain was drawn, it discovered even there a very splendid audience '. None of the actors, he adds, ' were guilty of the affectation to insert witticisms of his own '. The modern playwright has something to be thankful for.

CHAPTER XIV

In politics I am sure it is a holy maxim that some men
should be ruined for the good of others.

Theatre Politics

WHEN THE THEATRICAL season opened in the autumn of
1709, the theatre in the Haymarket, by the Lord Chamberlain's
edict, was given over once more exclusively to opera, and only
one company of straight actors remained in existence. Anne
found herself without choice, playing once more for Rich and
his partners at Drury Lane.

Rich saw his chance. Actors' Equity lay in the womb of the
future. Now that he possessed a monopoly, he thought he could
start paring down what he had to pay. He began with benefits
and proceeded to deduct, besides the usual charges, one-third
of the takings for the use of the Patent. He felt safe in so doing
since verbal agreements were still the order of the day.

He had reckoned without Anne's acumen and the contract
Vanbrugh had signed with her in the Lord Chamberlain's
office. On 4 March, the day after *The Beaux Stratagem* had
been played for her benefit and Rich had deducted one-third
of the receipts, she lodged a protest with the Lord Chamberlain:

Mrs Oldfield complains that when she acted at the Queen's
Theatre in the Haymarket she had an agreement for four pounds a
week salary and a benefit play every year, paying only out of the
receipts forty pounds, which agreement was entered in the Lord
Chamberlain's office. That upon my Lord's command and promise
of his protection and her being continued at the same salary and
terms of a benefit play at the Theatre Royal, she returned to act
there. That Mr Rich having consented to have a play acted for her
benefit the 3rd of this instant March, refuses to pay her the profits
exceeding forty pounds of such play, in absolutely demanding
seventy-one pounds for the use of the Patent, and insists on her
having only the remainder. Mrs Oldfield therefore humbly hopes
the Lord Chamberlain will use his authority to oblige Mr Rich to
keep the agreement she had with the Haymarket.

Why was it left to a woman, labouring under all the dis-abilities of her sex at that day, to be the first to beard the formidable Patentee, whose monopoly enabled him to deprive her of her living at will? Anne's intelligence told her that her position was not vulnerable since it was based in the final instance on Maynwaring's influence over the Whig party and at Court. On him she could, if the worst came to the worst, rely for her daily bread. Her example quickly inspired others of the Haymarket players.

Christopher Rich at first contented himself with retaliation in writing. Before the month was out, he and his partners had signed a reply to her protest, making these points:

On 20 March 1703, Mrs Oldfield had agreed with him to act at Drury Lane for five years at fifty shillings a week. No mention had been made of any benefit. This contract had not expired.

Any agreement with the Haymarket was no affair of his.

Since her return to Drury Lane, Mrs Oldfield had been paid four pounds a week, although until lately no actress had had over fifty shillings. This great salary with the benefit ate seriously into profits.

She had wanted *The Beaux Stratagem* for her benefit on 3 March. He had agreed. Forty pounds was deducted for charges while Mrs Oldfield received two-thirds of the remainder.

If Vanbrugh, hoping to entice actors to the Haymarket, took only forty pounds from benefit receipts, it must be remembered that Rich's expenses were greater than his.

Not content with this counterblast, Rich made his treasurer, Zachary Baggs, publish his somewhat nebulous accounts in the Press:

Mrs Oldfield had four pounds a week for fourteen weeks and one day only, as she left off acting after her benefit on March 17th [sic] and refused to assist others at their benefits.

She acted 39 times	£56	13	4
For her benefit	£62	7	8
And more by computation	£120	0	0
For sundries	£13	5	7
	£252	6	7

In January she was paid ten guineas to wear, during the whole season, a mantua petticoat that was given her for the stage. And she had for wearing on the stage a suit of boy's clothes, paid £2 10 0.

A play-bill refutes the statement that Anne refused to act in the benefits of her fellow-players, by showing her acting on 15 April, six weeks after her own benefit, on Mr Bickerstaffe's behalf. The fact that she tactfully left the stage empty for Mrs Barry and Mrs Bracegirdle on the occasion of Betterton's farewell may be at the bottom of this libel.

In other respects the season was unhappy. Queen Anne's consort Prince George of Denmark died (Arthur Maynwaring was given eighteen yards of superfine black cloth to attend his funeral) and the theatre was closed out of respect. Playhouses always faced a closure of six weeks for the death of royalty, besides the normal off-times of Holy Week and of Wednesdays and Fridays in Lent. When Drury Lane reopened, Mrs Oldfield was given two poor parts in two mediocre new plays. The management had begun ' to set their marks upon those who had distinguished themselves in the application for redress '. The parts handed out and plays chosen for revival were the weapons they chose.

Anne's crony, Mrs Porter, found she, too, had grounds for complaint. She had been twelve years on the stage and still was only paid two pounds a week. ' When several of the gentle-women that performed principal parts either neglected or were sick, she at a night's notice studied and played them perfect the next night.' She hoped to have the parts given her to play permanently, ' by which she might have gained reputation, when there was more time to study, but instead those parts were given to such as were below her '. She also had grievances because her benefit was put off until the town was empty, and over costumes and the dressing-room allotted her.

With delight Anne and Mrs Porter got wind of a private treaty into which the Lord Chamberlain was allowing Owen Swiney to enter. It was to be signed with the dissatisfied actors and the Haymarket was to be opened again for legitimate plays. Four leading actors were to go into management on a sharing basis with Swiney: Wilks, Cibber, Doggett and Mrs Oldfield. The avaricious Rich was to be put out of business by the official silencing of his theatre.

But women were not trusted in Anne's day. While the discussions over the partnership were going on, the character actor Thomas Doggett, professing the greatest admiration for Anne as an *artiste*, insisted that the business end would never be secure if more than one sex was admitted to the management. Considering that it was Mrs Oldfield's courage and common sense that had touched off the whole explosion, this may seem a little unfair. Anne, however, was always anxious to oblige her fellow-actors. When Doggett suggested that she should be offered ' a *carte blanche* ' instead of a share she readily agreed. She felt, she said, no slight and took his offer ' rather as a favour than a disobligation '. The *carte blanche* worked out at a guaranteed two hundred pounds a year with a benefit clear of charges. Anne's readiness to co-operate was remembered in the days of the syndicate's prosperity, when her salary was readily increased to three hundred guineas. Her benefit in good years brought her as much again.

At last preliminaries were settled. An actor (no name is given) saw the order signed in the Lord Chamberlain's office to silence the Theatre Royal. He hurried back to a rehearsal that Rich had called. The manager took him to task for being late. ' Sir,' said the player with a dramatic gesture, ' I have now no more business here than you have. In half an hour you will have neither actors to command nor authority to employ them.' Rich told him coldly that if he could not settle down to rehearse, he would lose his pay. At this moment a messenger from the Lord Chamberlain brought the fatal order. ' Read that o'er! ' declaimed the actor, echoing Shakespeare's advice to Cardinal Wolsey, ' And then to Breakfast with what Appetite you may.'

The contract between Owen Swiney, gentleman, and Anne Oldfield, spinster, of the parish of St Paul's, Covent Garden, is dated April 1709. Anne for a period of thirteen years undertakes to act any parts appointed her and to submit herself to all the rules. She promises not to appear at any other playhouse and to promote the interests of the company to the best of her ability. In return she is to get a yearly salary of two hundred pounds paid in nine instalments. If the Government orders a closure of the theatre for any time, a ' reasonable abatement ' is to be made in her salary. She is to have an annual vacation from 10 June to 10 September, but is not allowed to act in any other theatre during that period without Swiney's consent.

She signed her contract, spelling her Christian name with an ' e ', and sealed it with the head of a Roman emperor. Her signature was witnessed by Margaret Saunders her dresser and Arthur Maynwaring her lover who may be suspected of being a prime mover in these negotiations.

In the same month, Steele dedicated the opening number of his new paper *The Tatler* to Maynwaring in complimentary terms, which sound a little more sincere than the general run of such ascriptions:

> The grand purpose of the paper is to pull off the disguises of cunning, vanity and affectation. No man has a better judgment for the discovery, or a nobler spirit for the contempt, of such impostures than yourself, which qualities render you the most perfect patron for the author of these essays.

Maynwaring, who was at this time busy with his pen on the Sacheverell controversy, had served Steele in the matter of his appointment as official Gazetteer. At Sir Arthur's request Harley raised the salary from fifty to three hundred pounds, no small consideration with the ever-impecunious Irishman. When Steele went to thank the Tory Secretary, ' Pray sir, do not thank me,' said Harley, ' thank Mr Maynwaring.' During the essayist's brief career as a Civil Servant he tried, he said, to obey the rules of that body and ' to keep the paper very innocent and very insipid.'

CHAPTER XV

A honest man that is not quite sober, has nothing to fear.

ADDISON

Paper Warfare

ANNE WAS LIVING in New Southampton Street off the Strand. An idea of her way of life may be glimpsed from an advertisement that appeared in the Press:

IMOINDA, an actress at Drury Lane playhouse, having put off her London house and residing all the summer at her country seat, [some irony may be suspected] would, when she comes to town, board in some fashionable street with a respectable virtuous family that are people of sense and good conversation. She is willing to give four score pounds a year but expects a first floor furnished after the newest manner and a constant table of four hot dishes. If she brings an actress home with her from rehearsal, (for, poor souls, many of them want a dinner,) she'll allow for it and being anxious that everybody should know the worst of her – she does require a great deal of attendance and is a little passionate, but 'tis soon over.

Jane Rogers had recently played the part of Imoinda in Southerne's *Oroonoko* and may be suspected of inserting this notice. Eighty pounds a year was a good rent for her to pay for lodgings, but she would have to pay for a good address and a good table. Swift gave eight shillings a week for a first floor in Bury Street and considered that ' plaguy deep '. A whole house could be rented cheap, unfurnished: one with stables and a coach house ' in a genteel part of the town ' was advertised at fifty pounds a year. Another advertisement goes straight to the heart: ' To let. A new brick house, the rooms wainscotted and painted, lofty stories, large half-pace stairs that two people may go up abreast, in a new pleasant court planted with vines, jasmin and other greens.' But services were scanty. Some houses had water laid on in wooden pipes at a charge of about a pound a year. Otherwise water carriers and wells were the rule. Coal fires were the only means of heating and coal was expensive. Furniture was meagre: a table, high-backed chairs, a square settee, a couple of pictures, a looking-glass, window curtains, shelves for china (nearly all oriental), a tea-table, a screen – that was what the average sitting-room contained. During nearly the whole reign, war had exhausted the finances of the country and circumscribed its trade.

A more intimate picture of conditions is drawn by advertisements in the Press of Anne's day (the non-party *Daily Courant*, the Tory *Post Boy* and the Whig *Flying Post*) than by the scanty news items they feature. It is not a picture to attract the sentimentalist of the patches and powder school. Dental enormities are revealed by the daughter of the late Mr James Perrimore who lived, appropriately enough, at the sign of the *Hand and Mouth* in Long Acre, and advertises that she could clean teeth ' to admiration be they never so black '. She offers to ' take off the yellow and black scales that rots the teeth and decays the gums, although they have been so for many years '. Other *arcana* are hinted at by ' your Old Physician who desires you not to forget him. He cures all venereal diseases and the Great Pox with all its attending symptoms very cheap, pleasant and no neglect of business, in a few days. At *Lilly's Head*, over against Ludgate Church within Blackfriars Gateway, you will find relief in time of need.' Highwaymen, those heroes of romance, sound no more attractive in fact than the delinquent youth of to-day. Three notorious offenders are committed to Newgate Bar: one, Carr, ' his nose somewhat crooked and large '; John Webb, ' a tall man flat-nosed '; and William Fox, ' a middle-sized, down-looking fellow '. They were concerned in most of the recent London robberies and their victims are invited to come to the *White Bear* to inspect the three horses they were riding. That a certain carelessness may have facilitated their exploits, is suggested by an advertisement for three twenty-pound bank notes lost on Friday night ' by a gentleman very much in drink '. Two guineas reward and no questions asked, is promised to anyone who will bring them to Mr Robert Kerr, goldsmith in Cheapside. Perhaps Mr Kerr's condition may be excused by the announcement of ' the noblest new Obrion (Haut Brion) claret that was ever imported being bright, deep, strong and of a most delicious flavour ' for sale at fifty-four shillings a dozen.

This was the background on which Anne opened the autumn season of 1709 at the Haymarket in a revival of Farquhar's *Recruiting Officer* with her thirteen-year contract in her pocket.

★   ★   ★

Except for Mrs Centlivre's failure with *The Man's Bewitch'd*, she appeared in no new plays. In it she played Belinda, thought to be the steward's daughter who proves to have an Irish peer for father. Wilks, Doggett and Cibber were also in the cast. She added to her extensive comedy repertoire Vanbrugh's *Relapse*, Shadwell's *Epsom Wells* and Beaumont and Fletcher's *Scornful Lady*. In tragedy there was Banks's *Unhappy Favourite* and Southerne's *Oroonoko* where she replaced Mrs Rogers as Imoinda. An unusual genre for her was Doggett's farce *The Country Wake*. At her benefit, Etherege's *Man of Mode*, like the good Whig she was, she spoke a special epilogue ' recommending Liberty to the Beauties of Great Britain '.

Political feeling was at fever pitch. Uproar over the impeachment of Dr Sacheverell had been followed by the sensational dismissal of Godolphin's Whig ministry. Robert Harley, the moderate Tory, came to power. His younger brother, Edward, was Maynwaring's colleague as Auditor of the Imprest. That kept personal relations pleasant enough, but Maynwaring's temper was soured by his party's exodus into the wilderness. People had been pointing to him (Member now for West Looe) as a future minister and the falsification of his hopes made him bitter. No doubt his liver was affected by the ' corrosive qualities ' of champagne and burgundy. He was such good company that he was in request at every big party. ' This ruined his health and his sickness made him peevish.' Poor Anne, who did all she could to control his conviviality! ' From a very pleasant conversation, he grew insufferably peevish and humoursome.'

He vented his ill-temper on the Tory party. Writers like Prior, who deserted the Whigs, excited his disgust. Swift was another man of letters whom he detested. He said he was one of the wickedest wretches alive and regarded him as the most mercenary of political bravoes. Swift and Prior were prominent contributors to *The Examiner*, a newspaper started by Harley and Bolingbroke to air the Tory point of view. Maynwaring had already written essays for *The Tatler* and when a paper, not very enterprisingly called *The Whig Examiner*, came out ' to censure writings of others and to give all persons a re-hearing who have suffered under any unjust sentence of *The Examiner* ', he leapt into the breach, pen in hand.

Soon, in its pages, he was attacking fearlessly Swift's great pamphlet *The Conduct of the Allies*. He contributed a counter-blast, *Alcibiades to the Athenians*, quite forgotten by an ungrateful posterity. The paper did not long survive, but with *The Medley* Maynwaring took the torch from its stiffening fingers.

The first number he wrote entirely. So did he its third, sixth and tenth numbers. The labour proved too much for his constitution. About Christmas-time of the year 1710, he was taken very ill, ' complaining of a great cold and fearing it would touch his lungs '. Anne nursed him devotedly and had her reward: ' he came off the sourness the ill fortunes of his party and his ill health had engendered.'

She had had a hard year at the Haymarket. That summer she had not taken her usual holiday but had worked for the junior company that played during vacation. Money was short and Anne was contributing her full share. Events at the theatre now afforded her a little respite and the opportunity to devote her days and nights to her invalid.

A Tory lawyer with ' an enterprising head and a jovial heart ', William Collier, M.P. for Truro, had succeeded in ousting his brother attorney Rich from the occupation of Drury Lane and had won permission through his connection with the dominant Tories to restart operations there. His company was a weak one and poorly produced. But Barton Booth and his future wife, Mrs Santlow, scored a big success in a comedy by the younger Shadwell. Now, still using his pull with the Tories, Collier was allowed to do a deal with Swiney and his three partners. Drury Lane was exchanged for the Queen's Theatre in the Haymarket, where he meant to concentrate on opera. The triumvirate, Wilks, Cibber and Doggett, moved back to Drury Lane and took the company, including Mrs Oldfield, with them. There began the golden period and there Anne stayed for twenty years until her retirement.

The move from the Haymarket back to Drury Lane took

place at the end of 1710 and gave Anne leisure to nurse her lover through the worst of his illness. She did not appear until 8 January 1711, when she played Mrs Sullen in the never-failing *Beaux Stratagem*. For the rest of the season she played her regular repertory rôles, with apparently only one new play to diversify them, the anonymously written *Injur'd Love*, in which she, an abandoned wife, is marooned on a desert island, where needless to say she dresses as a man.

Under Anne's care Maynwaring grew better and resumed his labours on *The Medley*, once more writing with his own hand every number from the thirty-first to the thirty-eighth. The government paper *The Examiner* had little mercy on him, rather clumsily describing him as ' a dunce out of his element pretending to intermeddle with raillery and irony, whereas he has no manner of taste or understanding '. It pilloried one of his articles as the perfect reverse of Sir John Falstaff: not only dull in itself, but the cause of dullness in others. A writer in *The Examiner*, most probably the promiscuous Mrs Manley, complained of his journalistic tricks: ' " quoth he ", when he wished to banter; " my impious friend " when irony was his suit.' ' Irony ', she sneered, ' is not a work for such grovelling pens.'

An epilogue Maynwaring wrote for Anne to speak in Charles Johnson's *Wife's Relief* is nevertheless in his best vein. His respect for Anne's heart and brain had converted him to something like feminism:

> Could we a Parliament of women call,
> We'd vote such statutes as would tame ye all.
> First we'd resolve that all those married fellows
> Should banishment endure who durst be jealous. . . .
> Next, that those dull uncomfortable wights,
> Who sleep all morning and who sot a' nights,
> Should find, when they reel home with surfeits cloyed,
> Their tender wives with better friends employed.
> Lastly the man that breaks the marriage vow,
> (If any such in this good house you know,)
> For the first time should suffer a divorce;
> Adieu! those tempting words – for better and for worse!

Verily Anne had brought her Arthur a long way on the road to the twentieth century. It is perhaps significant that the play only ran three nights.

CHAPTER XVI

A dismal universal hiss.

MILTON

Anne Booed

ON THE FIRST Wednesday in January 1712, a middle-sized man with a squint in his lively black eye and a mouth that hung always half open, climbed painfully off the ship that had brought him through a storm to Harwich. This was Prince Eugene of Savoy, one of the great Captains of an age that produced the Duke of Marlborough, Charles XII of Sweden and Augustus the Strong. He did not linger long at Harwich and arrived in London at seven on Saturday night. Next morning he was granted a private audience by Queen Anne.

He had raced across Europe post-haste, to get Marlborough reinstated and the war prosecuted with vigour. But presently one of the lions at the Tower died, which Dr Partridge, ' the ingenious and worthy Astrologer ', foretold would presage the signature of peace.

Prince Eugene stayed on in London. On Monday 21 January he went to see the new play at Drury Lane. This was one of Mrs Centlivre's frequent failures, this time an adaptation from the Spanish, entitled *The Perplex'd Lovers*. Anne Oldfield was playing lead. She had also learnt and prepared to deliver an epilogue in honour of the Prince's visit to England. When word of her intention got round, she received threatening letters written her either by wicked Tories, who disliked Eugene's championship of Marlborough, or by perverse Whigs, who saw in him a rival to their hero. The management decided no risks must be taken, and on the first night at the end of the piece Anne stood mute in the wings. On the second night the Prince once more applauded from his Box. Anne took her considerable courage in her hands, stepped forth and addressed:

> That Stranger who has graced our land,
> Of Equal Fame for council and command:
> A Prince whose wisdom, valour and success
> A gazing World with acclamation bless. . . .

Prince Eugene was greatly moved. He sent round a gold snuffbox worth thirty-five pounds – to be given, not to the actress, but to the authoress. This lack of appreciation must be put down to the warrior's determined misogyny. He lived and died unmarried, ' a Mars without a Venus '.

Next night was the last the play was to see. This time the French Ambassador sat in the Box. Not to be outdone, and representing the opposing interests of Louis XIV, he sent Mrs Centlivre a second snuffbox. This one had a miniature on its golden lid and was said by the embassy servants to have cost fifty pistols in Paris.

(The gift of a snuffbox to a lady, however emancipated, may be thought inappropriate. But snuff was a novelty, eagerly sought after by both sexes. During Sir George Rooke's recent expedition to Cadiz, the army sacked Port St Mary and captured several thousand pounds' weight of snuff in tin canisters. On the way home the fleet, too, took fifty tons of raw snuff on its way from Havana. Improvidently, the sailors sold it at home ports for threepence a pound. The army more prudently kept their refined snuff and disposed of it gradually at high prices.)

On the night of the Prince's visit to *The Perplex'd Lovers*, was opened at Charing Cross the rival exhibition of two dwarfs: ' a little man three foot high and forty-two years of age, straight and proportionable every way.' Next door stood his wife, not three feet high and thirty years of age. She diverted the company by her ' extraordinary ' dancing. She was big with child, ' being the least woman that ever was with child in Europe '. Their little horse, one foot odd inches in height, performed ' several wonderful actions by word of command, being so small that it is kept in a box '. It is not recorded whether the family received the same august patronage as Mrs Centlivre's play.

★   ★   ★

The event of the year, and the cause of Anne being first hissed and then lauded to the skies, was a play from the pen of Ambrose Philips – Namby-Pamby, as his enemies nicknamed him. One of those enemies was Pope, whose jealousy, excited by Philips' pastorals, described in the Dunciad how Dulness ' saw slow Philips creep '. He was a fellow of St John's College,

Cambridge, who later contrived to get his Whig friend Addison to make him a magistrate. The salary was meagre and Ambrose applied for further preferment. ' I thought I had already provided for you ', said the Under-secretary irritably. ' Poetry is a trade I *cannot* live by ', retorted Philips. ' I scorn to owe my sustenance to another I *ought not* to live by.' Addison saw his point and got him the job of a Commissioner of the Lottery.

Undeterred by the fate of another University man's play (the short-lived Edmund Smith's even shorter-lived adaptation from Racine) Ambrose Philips determined to try his hand with the drama. He took Racine's *Andromaque* and turned it into *The Distrest Mother*. Once again he had the support of Addison, who had already shown his weakness for Racine translations. His powerful côterie went into action. Steele dropped in at Drury Lane to hear the play read. He came back vowing that some days later the passion of the characters still dwelt strongly in his imagination: ' I congratulate the age that they are at last to see truth and human life ' represented in heroic drama. The style and the sentiments of the play, he continues, are worthy of ' those of the highest education '. Then he permits himself to wallow in what can only be called sob-stuff:

It was the most exquisite pleasure to me to observe real tears drop from the eyes of those who had long made it their profession to dissemble affliction; and the player who read, frequently threw down the book, until he had given vent to the humanity which rose in him at some irresistible touches of the imagined sorrow.

This picture of the hard-boiled triumvirate and cast sitting round a table and crying their hearts out to hear a play read is surely one at which even the most incorrigible press agent would jib.

In order to make his characters truly great, goes on Steele, throwing his leg across his own hobby horse, the author realized the need of a ' foundation in superior thoughts and maxims '. He comes back to earth to admit an uneasy feeling that the play was not ' busy ' enough for the taste of the town, by which he presumably means there was not enough action. His final advice to the management is practical enough: every player should have a new costume.

Advance publicity did not end there. George Powell, that drunken but talented actor, sent a letter to *The Spectator*, which Steele may well have helped him write over a bottle or two:

I am appointed to act a part in the new play called *The Distrest Mother*. It is the celebrated grief of Orestes which I am called to personate but I shall not act it as I ought, for I shall feel it too intimately to be able to utter it. I was last night repeating a paragraph to myself, which I took to be an expression of rage and in the middle, there was a stroke of self-pity which quite unmanned me. Be pleased, sir, to print this letter that, when I am oppressed in this manner, a certain part of the audience may not think I am *out*; and I hope with this allowance to do it with satisfaction.

Meanwhile, there were difficulties in casting the play. The plot may be put baldly. To save her son Astyanax's life, Andromache promises to marry Pyrrhus, the man who killed her husband, Hector. Once she is married she means to kill herself. Just in time Hermione, the abandoned bride of Pyrrhus, instigates Orestes to kill him. Exit Orestes, pursued by the Furies. Orestes was to be played by Powell, Pyrrhus by Booth, Hermione by Mrs Oldfield and Andromache by Mrs Rogers. The last character is described by Steele as one:

who has behaved herself with heroic virtue in the most important circumstances of a female life, those of a wife, a widow and a mother. Domestic virtues concern all the world and there is none living who is not interested that Andromache should be an imitable character.

Any part so exemplary had clearly to be played by Jane Rogers, that exponent of feminine virtue on the stage; but as rehearsals proceeded the author was seen fidgeting and whispering to his friends. ' Mrs Oldfield ', he was convinced, ' was infinitely the more accomplished person for so capital a part.' And to Mrs Oldfield the part was transferred, while her friend Mrs Porter took over Hermione.

Jane Rogers was not the woman to take dethronement quietly. Her feud with Anne had flamed up long ago, when the younger and prettier woman had first joined the company. Oil was poured on the fire when Susan Verbruggen's parts were

H

distributed and Lady Lurewell, the heroine of Farquhar's *Constant Couple*, was given to Anne. To make it worse, Wilks, Jane's faithless lover, had voted for the younger actress. Jane lost her temper completely and cried that he had chosen Anne because she was his mistress. No one believed her, but to satisfy the jealous woman, Wilks is said to have staged a demonstration (it looks like a re-hash of the Bracegirdle story) casting the two rivals for Lady Lurewell on two successive nights and leaving it to the audience to decide emphatically in favour of Anne. In any case the critics rubbed salt into the wound by declaring that the contrast of the characters of Sir Harry Wildair and Lady Lurewell had gained Mr Wilks and Mrs Oldfield an ' immortal ' reputation.

Memory of this old humiliation boiled in Mrs Rogers's breast. To be supplanted again by Anne in this much publicized part of Andromache was the last straw. She resorted to strong-arm measures. While *The Distrest Mother* was in rehearsal, Jane raised ' a posse of profligates, fond of tumult and riot ', who made it nightly impossible for her rival to get a hearing. Addison went to see Anne as Celia in Beaumont and Fletcher's *Humourous Lieutenant* and was amazed to find her greeted on the rising of the curtain with ' a great concourse of cat-calls '. So outrageous became the conduct of Jane's claque of ' obscure people supporting the idle complaint of one rival actress against another ', that one night the management had to close the theatre and send away the audience, although there was one hundred and fifty pounds in the house. And so Anne's ordeal went on, night after night. She had grown accustomed to applause from all parts of the house, not least from the Gallery where ' Footmen and Prentice bawl in upper air '. Now every speech was interrupted with ' cat-calls and other damning instruments '.

At last Maynwaring thought the ordeal had gone on long enough: ' the Court hearing of it sent four of the royal messengers and a strong guard to suppress all disorders.' The management fearing, royal messengers or no, what might happen on the first night of the new play, took the precaution of packing the house. It had commissioned Steele to write a prologue which deprecated interruption:

> This piece presented in a foreign tongue
> When France was glorious and her monarch young,
> A hundred times a crowded audience drew,
> A hundred times repeated, still 'twas new. . . .
> Andromache, if in our author's lines,
> As in the great original she shines,
> Nothing but from Barbarity she fears,
> Attend with silence, you'll applaud with tears.

He need not have been anxious. Anne's performance touched the zenith of her tragic rôles. She met with ' universal and deserved applause ':

> No souls so senseless but what felt her flame,
> No breast so savage but her art could tame
> The snarling critic and the sneering beau
> Who neither show of worth or manners know,
> Awed by her looks their brutish din forbear
> And for a while a little human are.

John Hughes, playwright and musician, comments on the beauty of her voice – flexible, slow and modulated in a mournful tone. He quotes in particular her lines that exploit the melancholy of the ' o ' sound:

> I'll go, and in the anguish of my heart
> Weep o'er my child. If he must die, my life
> Is wrapt in his, I shall not long survive.
> 'Tis for his sake that I have suffered life,
> Groaned in captivity and outlived Hector.
> Yes, my Astyanax, we'll go together –
> Together to the realms of night we'll go,
> There to thy ravished eyes thy sire I'll show
> And point him out among the shades below. . . .

The play was a ' smash hit ', running eight consecutive nights and enjoying frequent revivals. Reading it to-day, this may seem to have been due not to the ' superior thoughts ', not even to the new costumes or the backing of the Whig highbrows. The stagecraft which came naturally to Philips and the careful plot-building which he took over from Racine was the secret. Moreover, he hit Augustan taste. In Steele's words, he gave the town the opportunity of witnessing a representation

of ' passion, sorrow, indignation, even despair itself, within the
rules of decency, honour and good-breeding! '

*   *   *

A certain Dr Reynardson, a don with a turn for versification,
' had his expectation roused to so high a pitch ' by what he
heard of the tragedy that he made an excursion to London to
see for himself. On his return he was commissioned by the
Dean of his college to write upon the art, rise and progress of
the English stage. The result was a poem, called *The Stage*,
which he dedicated to Addison, giving incidentally some description of how Powell, Booth and Mrs Oldfield acted.

Powell, to the delight of this very human don, had clearly
let himself go:

> When by Hermione's disdain undone,
> Distraction seizes Agamemnon's son,
> With artful rattling wheeze he draws his breath,
> Seems in the very agonies of death;
> He foams, he stares, he storms a madding note
> And all the fury thunders in his throat.

After this Barton Booth seemed tame, for all that Dr Reynardson has to say of his Pyrrhus is:

> A godlike air, quick eye, and accent smooth
> With all the manly graces shines in Booth.

But perhaps he struck the actor on one of his off-nights.
(Macklin who, dying perhaps at the age of one hundred and
four, had long memories, relates that on one of such nights
Booth was walking through his part as Pyrrhus, when suddenly
he noticed in the Pit the historian Stanyan, the intimate of
Addison and Steele; ' calling for a glass of wine and water he
proceeded to electrify the audience and the other actors ', and,
it is to be hoped, the historian.)

It is when the author of *The Stage* reaches the performance
of Anne Oldfield that for a couple of lines he is very nearly
stirred into poetry:

Should Oldfield then, the bright-eyed Oldfield, join
Her complicated charms, her form divine,
Should she like Hector's widow as of late
Mourn her Astyanax's double fate,
All, all would love her like Achilles's son,
All would like him be taken, all like him undone . . .

Another figure, more famous than the college don, if less substantial, visited *The Distrest Mother*. This was Sir Roger de Coverley.

The old Tory knight, says Addison, had not been to a play for twenty years but had a great mind to see the new tragedy. He wanted to know who this distressed mother was. Hearing that she was Hector's widow, he remarked that Hector was a very brave man and that he had read his life at school at the end of the dictionary. He arranged for Addison to meet him about four o'clock, so that they might be at the theatre before it was full. As soon as the candles were lit, Sir Roger stood up and looked about him ' with that pleasure which a mind, seasoned with humanity, naturally feels in itself at the sight of a multitude of people, who seem pleased with one another and partake of the same common entertainment '.

He followed the play attentively and kept on remarking that he could not imagine how it would end, a tribute to Philips' power of suspense. On Booth's entrance, the old man whispered that he did not believe the King of France himself had a better strut. At one moment he was much concerned for Mrs Oldfield, at another time for Mrs Porter, and was greatly puzzled to think what would happen to Booth. When Anne refused to listen to Pyrrhus's entreaties, Sir Roger whispered that he was sure she would never give in to him, adding aloud from his own experience: ' You can't imagine, sir, what it is to have to do with a widow.' When Booth threatened to leave Anne, ' Ay, do if you can!' the knight muttered. For a time he brooded on this scene and at the end of the act, showed where his thoughts had lingered: ' these widows ', he said, ' are the most perverse creatures in the world.' During the interval, he showed he did not belong to the school of thought that to-day reverences current twentieth-century poetic drama. ' Pray,' said he, ' you that are a critic, is the play according to your dramatic rules,

as you call them? Should your people in tragedy always talk to
be understood? Why, there is not a single sentence in this play
that I do not know the meaning of! ' The next act had begun
before Addison had thought out an answer.

Sir Roger was full of admiration for Mrs Oldfield, but a little
puzzled by one of the boy pages who, in accordance with the
tradition of the day, carried her train. Him he took for Astyanax
her son: a fine child, he declared. Mrs Porter's exit with a
denunciation of Booth on her lips brought down the house.
' On my word,' commented the knight, ' a notable young
baggage! '

In the last interval, the audience began to discuss the acting.
Hearing Powell praised, Sir Roger chipped in and said he
found Orestes' friend Pylades, played by Mills, a very sensible
man. ' And let me tell you,' he added, ' though he speaks but
little, I like the old fellow in whiskers [he meant Bowman,
playing Phœnix] as well as any of them.' In the final act Sir
Roger listened attentively to Powell's description of the killing
of Pyrrhus, and remarked that he was glad it was done off stage.
When Orestes, haunted by the Furies, goes mad, the old man
looked serious and drew a moral about a guilty conscience,
adding that the actor looked as if he saw something.

A footnote to the knight's visit is provided by a letter in a
subsequent *Spectator*. This purports to be written by a member
of the audience who sat near Sir Roger and listened with
pleasure to his comments. That is, until the end of the piece.
When the time came for Anne's epilogue, which after the
fashion of the day was written in a humorous vein to dispatch
the audience in a happy mood:

> But why, you'll say, was all this grief expressed
> For a first husband laid long since at rest?
> Why so much coldness to my kind protector?
> Ah! ladies! Had you known the good man Hector!

the letter-writer hoped to see Sir Roger follow his practice and
go out before the epilogue started; ' having paid down my
half-crown and made a fair purchase of so much of the pleasing
melancholy as the poet's art can afford me, I am willing to
carry some of it home with me.' To his disappointment he saw

the old knight rooted to his seat and ' as much satisfied with
Mrs Oldfield's gaiety as he had been before with Andromache's
greatness, pleased to find at last that, after all the tragical
doings, everything was safe and well '. The correspondent was
disgusted at the change of mood. His soul during the action of
the play had been worked up to the highest pitch, and the
facetious epilogue extinguished his ardour.

Next week his attitude was questioned in a second letter:

Sir, I am amazed to find an epilogue attacked in your last
Friday's paper, which has been so generally applauded by the town
and received such honours as were never before given to any in an
English theatre. The audience would not permit Mrs Oldfield to
go off the stage till she had repeated it twice. The second night the
noise of *ancora* was as loud as before and she was again obliged to
speak it twice. The third night it was called for a second time and
in short, contrary to all other epilogues, which are dropped after
the third presentation of the play, this has already been repeated
nine times. . . . The moment the play ends, Mrs Oldfield is no more
Andromache, but Mrs Oldfield, and though the poet had left
Andromache stone-dead upon the stage, Mrs Oldfield might still
have spoke a merry epilogue.

This second writer loved to be sent home to bed in a good
humour and could only advise his opponent, if he was resolved
to be inconsolable, to follow his old custom and, when he had
had his half-crown's worth of gloom, to slink out before the
epilogue began.

Anyone who reads the epilogue will feel that its prodigious
success was due less to its author (Eustace Budgell officially, but,
according to current rumour, his cousin Joseph Addison) than
to Anne. Her natural comedy, the music of her voice, the
elegance of her dress, the effective use of eye and gesture to
point every double meaning, all combined to put over the
humorous epilogue.

So Anne triumphed alike in the character of Andromache
and in the rôle of herself. Before long Jane Rogers, tired of her
hopeless struggle, migrated to the new theatre in Lincoln's Inn
Fields that Rich's son opened. Another few years and she
disappeared. She died or left the stage.

CHAPTER XVII

The world's an inn and death's the journey's end.

DRYDEN

Death of a Satirist

IN THE SUMMER of 1712, in spite of Anne's ' great care and concern ', her lover had a relapse. He had for some time been pressing the Lord Chamberlain to provide him with better office facilities. With Edward Harley he signed a memorandum pointing out that, as Auditor of the Imprest, he had in his charge vouchers for many millions of pounds which had to be ' preserved and disposed in such order that recourse may be had to them on any occasion '. The rooms at his service, he complained, were too small; but nothing happened for some time until at last Sir Christopher Wren, Surveyor General, suggested the use of the Whitehall lodgings of the late Master of the Household. This recommendation the Lord Chamberlain whittled down. He thought the three-story annex to the lodgings should be big enough. Had Maynwaring known how short a time he had left to occupy it, he might have cared less.

The weather was hot and Anne moved her patient to the village of Hampstead, where there was a chalybeate spring which was opened at the beginning of every June. Accommodation was advertised for ' water drinkers of both sexes and very good music for dancing '. It is unlikely that Maynwaring felt well enough to take any pleasure in the music or the dancing, but at least he was able to see his friends, for the summer headquarters of the Kit-cat Club were at the Flask inn.

Hampstead did him little good and after a time he was moved to the village of Paddington. By now his illness was diagnosed as tubercular. The treatment of the day was sound. It prescribed simple diet, taking the air and riding. Maynwaring dutifully rode every fine morning, but daily his decline became more visible. He struggled on with his journalism. One day in September he rode over to the Duchess of Marlborough's house at St Albans. There he wrote the number of *The Medley* that was to be his last. That evening he walked too late in the garden. He caught a ' great cold '. Anne sent for the great Whig physicians, Sir Samuel Garth and Sir Richard Blackmore. Both dabbled in literature; both were personal friends of the patient. The portly Garth was a member of the Kit-cat Club. In its book of Minutes, there had been an entry some years back: ' Alexander the Great played by gentlemen. Dressers for the ladies, Mrs Bracegirdle and Mrs Oldfield, by consent of the Earl of Scarsdale and Mr Maynwaring, who are to speak the prologue and epilogue both writ by Doctor Garth.' The gaiety of those days was gone. Sir Samuel and Sir Richard shook their distinguished heads and expressed small hope of their patient's recovery – indeed it was his own opinion that this great cold would ' finish what his former illness had begun '.

Arthur's sister Grisel was a Tory with little confidence in Whig medicine. She sent for her party's doctor, John Radcliffe, whose fees went after his death to found the Radcliffe Infirmary. Dr Radcliffe was renowned for his candour. On the death of Queen Mary, he was summoned to minister to her afflicted sister, Princess Anne. He was discovered over a bottle in a tavern in St James's; returning a message that the Princess was only suffering from the vapours, he ordered another bottle. Next day, on presenting himself at the Palace, he cannot have been surprised to be told he was superseded as Royal Physician by Dr Gibbons. Some years later, no doubt as the consequence of some fresh outburst of candour, he had to summons an apothecary of St Martin's Lane for spitting in his face at Tom's Coffee House. The celebrated comment is ascribed to Radcliffe, as he watched workmen filling in the soil over a badly laid drain: ' Mine is not the only faulty work the earth hides.' Nevertheless, he amassed a large fortune and was notorious for a resplendently gilded coach and a liaison with Miss Tempest, a lady-in-waiting half his age.

This outspoken physician was called by Grisel Maynwaring to her brother's bedside. He had been adjured by Robert Harley, the Tory Treasurer, ' Pray doctor, take care of that gentleman as one of the most valuable lives in England.' Maynwaring was grateful for his opponent's good will and promised, if he recovered, he would never attack him again.

Radcliffe laughed and promised the invalid he would be on his feet in two or three weeks. Before he left he prescribed a new treatment.

Maynwaring lay back. In his heart he felt he was doomed, and on 27 September he sent for a lawyer to meet him at Anne's house in Southampton Street. In spite of the sale of his ancestral estate and the substantial salary his post brought him, he had only some three thousand pounds to bequeath. He left a thousand pounds to his sister and the remainder to be divided equally between his son by Anne and Anne herself. If Arthur should die before he was twenty-one, the whole was to go to Arthur's mother, who was also named as executrix. Maynwaring wrote the will in his own hand and kept the provisions to himself. It was witnessed by Owen Swiney, theatre manager, William Buckeridge, apothecary, and Maynwaring's servant, Thomas Wood, who after his master's death worked in the box office at Rich's new theatre in Lincoln's Inn Fields.

Dr Radcliffe's prognosis was faulty. His treatment, which Sir Samuel and Sir Richard naturally criticized, did not prove effective. ' All the great people of both sexes who had the happiness of his acquaintance ', came to see Maynwaring, but only a few were admitted. Under the chaperonage of Grisel, Queen Anne herself paid him the honour of a visit to his bedside. She could find no words to utter and, most tactlessly, subsided into tears. This drew tears, too, in his weakened state, from the dying man. He struggled to express his gratitude for the royal condescension, which was the deeper because there had been ' a slight misunderstanding between him and this great lady ', over the new office. A few hours later he died in the arms of his devoted servant, Thomas Wood. It was 14 November 1712. He was only forty-four.

Anne was broken-hearted. Her only touch with her dying lover had been through his servant, Thomas Wood, for Grisel's presence excluded her from his bedroom. She had to go on with rehearsals by day and nightly performances at Drury Lane. How she got through them without breaking down on the stage she never knew. Bitterly she wished she was married and possessed the rights of a wife. It was the most miserable time of her life.

In his will Arthur had directed that she should arrange his funeral. She had him buried in the church at Chertsey, alongside his father and grandfather, with the utmost simplicity, ' answering more to his modesty than to his merit. He never affected pomp, living.' She thought the best memorial to him was the care of his seven-year-old son, whose future had always occasioned his father great anxiety. ' What will become of the boy when I am gone? ' he had exclaimed the last time she saw him, thinking of the poor provision he was able to make. It was some consolation that young Arthur was so like his father ' in feature and vivacity '; but he was perhaps more fortunate in his mother. She gave him a good education and, when he was old enough, bought him a commission in the Guards. In her will she was to leave him five thousand pounds, five times the amount his father had bequeathed.

There is a story that to capitalize her own ' distressed motherhood ', she used to take the fatherless child with her on the stage as she spoke Andromache's epilogue. If she did, she must be pardoned; for at this period in her life she needed all the sympathy from the public she could arouse. Besides her private enemies, Jane Rogers and Grisel Maynwaring, every Tory hand was lifted against so popular a protagonist of Whig sentiment. A few weeks after Maynwaring's death, Mrs Manley, who already in the summer had discoursed delicately of ' the disorders of a broken constitution ', launched a full-throated attack on the dead man and on his living mistress. Reminding the readers of *The Examiner* that Maynwaring had ' got to be poor in the Jacobite cause and then resolved to grow rich and honest in the cause of the Whigs ', she accused him of abandoning at the end of his life all religion and morality. Throwing away honour and the natural affection he owed a devoted sister, he made his mistress, she gibed, his executrix and principal legatee. This charge was calculated to hurt. The reputation of actresses gave Anne's ill-wishers grounds to criticize her for displacing Grisel as executrix, nor could they believe how loyally she was fulfilling the trust. Worse was to follow. The immaculate Manley, herself kept by an alderman, ended with an innuendo that Maynwaring had diverted to his own use public funds and had bestowed these ill-gotten

gains, the monumental legacies of Whig honesty, on a celebrated actress, 'who is too much admired upon the stage to
have any enquiry made into her conduct behind the curtain'.

This contemptible attack on the dead was not the only
wound that Anne in this time of grief had to endure. A whispering campaign (Jane Rogers's tongue was a bitter one)
started the rumour that Arthur Maynwaring's death was due
to ' the remains of a venereal distemper '. This particularly foul
insinuation was calculated to harm alike the dead man's
memory and his mistress's standing with her public. In his
lifetime there had long been current a story of some such
infection. He denied it, admitting ' that in the reign of King
William he had made an unfortunate sally in an amour, which
gave him a slight taint at Paris in 1698. That he was only
patched up there but afterwards perfectly cured at London,
since which time he had never had any such misfortune.'

Anne was determined to vindicate her lover's good fame and
to establish her own clean bill of health. With the directness of
the century she had the body opened by two surgeons, Mr
Bussière and Mr Browne, in the presence of two physicians,
Dr Beeston and Dr West, and of the apothecary Buckeridge.
The result of this post-mortem was eminently satisfactory. The
unanimous verdict was that no trace of venereal disease existed
but that death was due to tuberculosis. As a Whig contemporary
put it, ' When he was opened up, he was found as sound as his
judgement '.

A champion, believed to be Sir Robert Walpole, came to the
rescue of his dead friend's memory, and in a long *Defence of
Mr Maynwaring in a Letter to a Friend* rebutted the charges in
The Examiner. Another Whig well-wisher published an epitaph.
Arthur Maynwaring's

learning was without pedantry; his wit without affectation; his
judgement without malice; his friendship without interest; his zeal
without violence. In a word he was the best subject, the best friend,
the best relation, the best master, the best critic and the best political
writer in Great Britain.

His claim to the last distinction in an age which produced
Matthew Prior and Jonathan Swift may be thought exaggerated. But then they both wrote in the Tory interest.

CHAPTER XVIII

The great, the important day . . . of Cato.
ADDISON

Cato

AMID HER tribulation Anne was able to find consolation in
the thought that she was now carrying her dead lover's child,
conceived before the fatal stroll in the garden at St Albans. She
was, moreover, kept hard at work, an opiate for which she may
not have felt enough gratitude. Besides her daily appearances
in the stock repertory – the everlasting Andromache, Congreve's ' jill-flirt ' Angelica and the rest – she was, at the very
moment of her Arthur's death, rehearsing Cibber's new tragedy
which Ambrose Philips's success had provoked. This was an
adaptation of Corneille's *Le Cid* under the title of *Ximena or the
Heroick Daughter*.

Steele went to a rehearsal on purpose to tell his readers how
far the piece was a faithful translation and how much original
work Cibber had put into it. In his report he gives no very
clear solution. He could not fail to notice that the end of the
play, where Ximena (Mrs Oldfield) is happily married, was
Cibber's own idea. He had a word with the adapter, who confessed that he was working to please the spectator at the
playhouse rather than the student in his study. Steele found the
company so anxious for the success of their fellow actor,
rehearsing with ' such grace, emphasis and force ', that it was
no easy matter to judge the *play*. Mrs Oldfield, as the Heroick
Daughter, ' had so just a conception of her part that her action
made what she spoke appear decent, just and noble '. Anyone
who contrives to struggle through *The Heroick Daughter* will take
this as the very highest tribute to Anne's art. Cibber's verse is
unbearably flat, though even the most inspired English translation of Corneille makes pretty heavy weather.

The entire cast gathered round Steele in an attempt to
convince him that the play raised ' passions of terror and com-

passion ' and that the whole production was ' very artful and
surprising '. Steele, as a playwright, did not much appreciate
the actors' valuation, ' having the same disdain as physicians
and lawyers have when attorneys and apothecaries give advice '.
Cibber contributed his views on the art of holding an audience
in a lecture on the technique of acting: ' the artful management
of the look, voice and gesture.' Steele made his escape, admitting tactfully, if vaguely, that *The Heroick Daughter* appeared
in rehearsal ' a moving entertainment wrought out of a great
and exemplary virtue '.

In the upshot Cibber was proved to know his business. The
play pleased the audience, ran six consecutive nights, was
revived the following March for Anne's benefit and later appeared new-dressed and revised. If it failed to satisfy the critics,
the author did not care, leaving John Dennis to his opinion
that ' Mr Cibber's *Heroick Daughter* may be, for ought I know,
more heroical than the daughter of Corneille. But there is this
difference, that Corneille's is beautiful and spiritual and Mr
Cibber's ugly and insipid.' Cibber used to console himself,
when reading onslaughts of this nature, with a philosophical
' Time is the Judge '. Unfortunately for his reputation he was
right.

The fashion for classical French tragedy was now firmly in
the saddle, and *Cinna's Conspiracy*, an anonymous translation of
Corneille's *Cinna*, followed hard. It is usually ascribed to the
same indefatigable pen. Apart from the fact that Mrs Oldfield
played lead, as was her habit in her brother-actor's plays, there
is little save ignoble verse to identify it as Cibber's. The translation ran three nights and was never seen again. Anne shrugged
off the labour she had put into it, and turned to the next play.

Already Joseph Addison had noted the triumph that attended
classical tragedy in Philips's hands. In his drawer lay an excursion into Roman historical drama under the title of *Cato*.
He touched it up and showed it to Alexander Pope. The poet
gave his sincere opinion. Its best chance of adding to his
friend's reputation was in book form. It was well written but
not dramatic. This cold douche did not deter the would-be
playwright. He wanted the opinion of someone more intimately
connected with the theatre. Maynwaring had not yet caught

the fatal cold and Addison shared the general belief in his critical judgment. But again, Maynwaring's verdict was unfavourable. He did not consider Cato a suitable character for a hero of tragedy. Heroic drama demanded a man of action whose character was wrecked on some great human failing. Cato was a Stoic and his creed made him face disaster passively and with calm. As for the love interest (Juba, the Numidian prisoner, is in love with Cato's daughter, Marcia. So is the treacherous Roman senator Sempronius, who disguises himself as Juba and is killed by him), these scenes were wholly subsidiary, while the meat of the play lay in the part of Cato and his glorification of the old Roman – and English – spirit. With his mind on Mrs Oldfield for Marcia, Maynwaring saw the disadvantages of this subordination.

Still undiscouraged, the author took his first-born to John Hughes, playwright, musician and contributor to his *Spectator*. Hughes was a great admirer of *The Distrest Mother* and he divined in *Cato* an even greater success. Soon Addison was apologizing to Pope that though personally he shared the poet's opinion of his play, some particular friends of his, whom he could not disoblige, insisted on its production. These friends, convinced Whigs, were not blind to the state of political feeling. The Whig war was about to be wound up by the Tory Treaty of Utrecht. They were astute enough to see how political feeling could be exploited to the advantage of the play.

At last *Cato* went into rehearsal. Addison was too nervous or too excited to read the play to the assembled actors. He delegated the task to Cibber. So well did Cibber read that Addison, with all the amateur's impetuosity, insisted that he be cast for the rôle of Cato. Cibber himself was flattered and would not have been loath to accept, but Wilks intervened and opted for the Tory Barton Booth, who thus was entrusted with a part written as the rallying point of the opposite camp. Without hesitation Anne was cast to play his daughter Marcia, ' Marcia sighing for her Juba's heart ', and Wilks was given the part of Juba.

Rehearsals went on throughout Lent. One Friday a deaf, middle-aged parson, his dark clothes spotlessly clean, his eyes azure-blue and shrewd, came punctually at ten o'clock, the hour fixed for rehearsal, with half a dozen other curious spectators. This was the formidable Dean Swift. He stood on the stage and his presence brought small comfort to the cast. ' It was foolish enough ', ran his subsequent comment, ' to see the actors prompted every minute and the poet directing them; and the drab that acts Cato's daughter *out* in the midst of a passionate part and then calling out " What's next?".'

Anne was by now heavily pregnant and her condition may have prompted the clergyman's sneer. But he was always too ready with the epithet. A couple of years earlier he had attended an opera rehearsal at which he heard Margherita de l'Epine sing with another ' drab and a parcel of fiddles '. A more courteous visitor was Anne's old friend and rival in love, Susan Centlivre. So charmed was she with Anne's performance that she scribbled some commendatory verses on the fly-leaf of a book she had borrowed from the actress, a work of popular science by a nephew of Corneille, forbiddingly entitled *Plurality of Worlds.*

> Plurality of Worlds! [she wrote] Such things may be,
> But I am best convinced by what I see. . . .
> Now Cupid skilled in Mysteries profound,
> Points where more certainty of Worlds abound:
> Bright Globes that strike the Gazer with Surprise
> For they are Worlds of Love and in Ophelia's Eyes.

Ophelia, of course, was a popular sentimentalization of Oldfield.

The first night was fixed for Tuesday in Easter Week. The date was well chosen, as theatres had been closed during Holy Week and the appetite of the audience was keen-set. Addison announced that he would give the proceeds of his third-night benefit to the actors. All the front boxes had been taken for a fortnight. Steele took precautions to provide a first-night claque: ' a crowd of silly persons ', said the Tory Press tartly, ' drawn up under the leading of the renowned Ironsides and appointed to clap at his signals.'

He need not have troubled. The most awful and brilliant audience that ever graced a theatre assembled, so the triumvirate later told the veteran Macklin. All the ambassadors of foreign powers had boxes. Whigs and Tories were ranged on opposite sides of the house. The author, with two or three friends (among them George Berkeley, future philosopher and Bishop of Cloyne), sat in a side box. He had taken the precaution to provide a table laden with burgundy and champagne. Its object was to ' support his spirits in the concern he was under ', though it admittedly provided ' very pleasant refreshment ' to the whole party between the acts. In the next box sat Harley, recently created Lord Oxford, the Tory Treasurer. Addison's party kept a keen eye on his reactions.

The curtain rose. Enter Wilks in the make-up of Juba, to speak the prologue, wearing, like all the cast, a splendid new costume. Wilks was a warm Whig and the best prologue speaker that ever trod the English stage. (It is more likely that Macklin derived this opinion from Wilks than from Cibber, whose views on the subject have already been quoted.) On this occasion Alexander Pope had given him good matter to declaim. The lines about Cato giving ' his little senate laws ' and on proud Cæsar, ' ignobly vain and impotently great ', are over-familiar, but the final lines, which deal with theatre problems of the day, are less hackneyed:

> With honest scorn the first-famed Cato viewed
> Rome learning arts from Greece whom she subdued;
> Our Scene precariously subsists too long
> On French translations and Italian song.
> Dare to have sense yourselves, assert the stage,
> Be justly warmed with your own native rage. . . .

As the play proceeded each point was underlined with ecstatic applause from Whig and Tory alike. Every time the word ' liberty ' occurred, there was a rapturous burst of Whig clapping, drowned by Tory cheering to show that their party set no lower value on the commodity. The Tory Treasurer was observed in his box applauding continuously. Between the acts some enthusiastic Whig started a collection with four guineas in a purse for the triumphant Cato. The purse went round the boxes and soon was heavy with gold. Taken to the Greenroom it was presented to Barton Booth in the name of the Whigs of the British Empire for having declaimed so well in the cause of ' Expiring Liberty '. Not to be outdone, in the next interval

I

Bolingbroke, the Tory negotiator of the peace, sent for the actor and from the stage gave him another purse of fifty guineas. This, he explained, was in the name of *all* Her Majesty's loyal subjects for having defended so well the cause of liberty against ' a perpetual dictator '. The comparison of Marlborough with Julius Cæsar brought down the Tory half of the house. For the Whigs, Sir Samuel Garth remarked that Cato would have something to live on when he was dead. The rotund doctor had written the facetious epilogue which had to be spoken by Mrs Porter. Anne Oldfield's figure was thought too unshapely to permit her to undertake her usual task. Nor would Garth's opening lines have looked appropriate:

> What odd fantastic things we women do,
> Who would not listen when young lovers woo
> But die a maid. . . .

At the end of the play, the author was generously applauded by both political parties. The future Bishop of Cloyne thought he had performed a very difficult task with great success, having introduced the noblest ideas of virtue and religion upon the stage with the greatest applause. The notices were most favourable. As might be expected, the Whig *Flying Post* dotted the i's:

How wonderfully [it ended] must this example work up the passions of a generous Briton! But alas! such are these unhappy times that with too, too many does the character of Sempronius agree, who shall outwardly pretend mighty zeal for liberty, but are inwardly wishing for a popish pretender and an arbitrary government.

John Dennis's criticism was, as nearly always, just:

Probability ought certainly to reign in every tragical action but it ought not to exclude the wonderful. Here are none of these beautiful surprises. I sit with indolence from the opening of the play to the very catastrophe.

Voltaire, who was to see the play when he came to England a few years later, was more enthusiastic: he thought it the only ' reasonable ' tragedy in the English language and the part of Cato one of the finest on any stage. He translated the speech, ' Cato, thou reasonest well . . .' (which sometimes received an encore during performance) into French and declared it as good as anything Shakespeare ever wrote. In spite of his prejudice against that dramatist, he had to admit: ' Addison had more taste, but the abyss between taste and genius is immense. Shakespeare had an amazing genius, but no taste.'

Every schoolboy is to-day encouraged to sneer at the frigidities of *Cato*, but its sincerity is oftener overlooked. In its own day it received the ' greatest approbation of any play that has been represented on the theatre in this or any preceding age '. The published work was in great demand. The women who sold oranges and fruit in the Park offered it to the coaches as they drove by.

On the stage it ran a record thirty-five nights and was good, says George Berkeley, for another month. It was poor Anne's fault that it had to be taken off since she ' could not hold out any longer '. She had for some time had a midwife waiting for her in the wings, which, remarked the philosopher demurely, is surely very unbecoming the character of Cato's daughter.

The last night was on Saturday 9 May. Between that date and the end of June, when the play was taken to Oxford, Anne gave birth to a baby which, to her great grief, did not live. Either the father's precarious health at the time of conception or Anne's manifold griefs and labours during the period of pregnancy were to blame.

There had been some doubt over the Oxford experiment. It was felt that that erudite audience would prefer the work of Jonson or Shakespeare to such modern fare. But the author was a product of Magdalen, where Addison's Walk may still be trod. It was decided to take the risk with a play that was ' the flower of a plant raised in that learned garden '. The venture exceeded all hopes; box office receipts were good and it was found possible to double every actor's salary, as well as to subscribe fifty pounds to the repair of St Mary's Church. On leaving, the company was publicly thanked by the Vice-Chancellor, with honourable mention of the decency and order they had observed. The eighteenth century did not expect too much of its actors.

CHAPTER XIX

. . . what creatures widows are in weeping for their husbands and then leaving off; but I cannot wonder at it, the cares of this world taking place of all other passions.

S. PEPYS

Backstage

UNDER ANNE OLDFIELD'S reign dawned the golden age of Drury Lane. That theatre was called ' the school of politeness, where persons of the front rank might have learnt such behaviour as would have added to their dignity '. Much of this elegance derived from the brilliance of Anne's comedy playing:

> Oldfield whose every action had a tongue,
> Graceful her air, her speech melodious song. . . .

but the hard work of the management deserves mention. After his triumph in *Cato*, Barton Booth took the place of Doggett to complete the triumvirate. He found the post no sinecure. Apart from actors there were one hundred and forty names on the pay roll. ' Among such numbers,' says one of the managers, ' it will be no wonder if a great many of them are unskilful, idle and untractable. All which tempers are to be led or driven, watched and restrained by the continual care and patience of the managers.' The Lord Chamberlain's rules required them to meet once a week. They examined accounts, paid bills[1] and salaries; they decided, and their decision had to be unanimous, on the increase or reduction of the pay of musicians, singers, dancers, scene painters, stage carpenters, scene shifters, door keepers and the rest of the staff, one hundred and forty strong. They had to settle whom to sack. They signed orders for all purchases over one pound. They ordered and helped design new costumes and held the scales between the competitors who wanted to wear them. They chose and cast old plays for revival and read new scripts for production, ' though there are seldom one of those plays in twenty ', says a manager pessimistically,

---

[1] It took the triple signature of Wilks, Cibber and Booth to authorize the one item: May 8, 1714 for one white chamber pott for Mr Bullock. 00.00.06.

' which upon hearing proves to be fit for it '. The disappointed author had then to be got rid of, a task described as ' both disagreeable and difficult '.

Beside administrative duties, one manager was told off to attend rehearsals for two or three hours every morning. Without such supervision, rehearsals tended to be ' but a rude meeting of mirth and jollity '. During the first three days of rehearsing a new play, the manager directed the reading of the book. Then the actors rehearsed, part in hand. Soon a date was fixed for everyone to be word perfect, when the producer concentrated on entrances and exits, emphasis and attitudes. The routine has not altered much in two hundred and fifty years, but in the good old days the producer had power to dismiss and fine ' the negligent and worthless '. His duties did not, as to-day, end with the first few nights. One or more of the managers had to superintend the nightly production, whether he was playing or not. In addition, novices had to be given singing and dancing lessons. For his pains and for his expenses in clothes, wigs, linen and lace, a manager received one and a half guineas a day.

It was not to be expected that the triumvirate would escape criticism. Much of it came from unlucky playwrights. There was John Dennis, whose plays were as bad as his reviews were good. ' The theatre is now in the hands of players: illiterate, unthinking, unjust, ungrateful and sordid.' Sordid was his favourite epithet for the management, whose ' sordid love and greediness of gain contributes to the corrupting of their understandings. For when a foolish play happens to have a run, their sordid temper inclines them to believe it good: it immediately becomes a stock play.' It is the age-old quarrel of the highbrow writer with the commercial standards of the box office.

Of course, it was far easier for an author to get a play produced if he was on the right side in politics. The seasons that opened after the production of *Cato* until Anne's illness in the winter of 1720, saw thirteen new plays in which she acted and a dozen more in which she did not. Of the former list, nearly all written by writers of established reputation, two were by Rowe, a fervent Whig; two more by Mrs Centlivre, who was of the same creed; one by Addison himself and one each by John

Hughes and Edward Young, both prominent in Addison's circle; one was by Thomas Killigrew, gentleman of the bedchamber to George, Prince of Wales; one was by Colley Cibber, actor-manager and a warm Whig; two were by Charles Johnson, the bosom friend of Robert Wilks, actor-manager; one was by Gay, a less steadfast Whig and moreover tarred with the collaboration of Pope and Arbuthnot; while only one was by an avowed Tory, the veteran Southerne, whose past reputation meant he could not be refused. The circumstances may be paralleled by the 'twenties and 'thirties of the present century when all the intelligentsia was triumphantly Left wing; not for nothing was Drury Lane known as the Whig house, in distinction from the Tory house in Lincoln's Inn Fields.

Anne was still under her late lover's influence and she remained enthusiastically Left wing. For all her success, she remained at heart a simple person. ' She was always ready ', says Cibber, ' to have all the helps another could possibly give her. It was a hard matter to give her any hint she was not able to take and improve.' She was very tractable and unpresuming. In spite of a quite unsupported allegation that she held herself aloof from her fellow-actors, according to the prompter Chetwood she was always affable and good-natured.

Rowe now wrote for her the two great ' she-tragedies ' *Jane Shore* and *Lady Jane Grey* which head the thirteen new plays Anne graced during these busy years.

*   *   *

A present-day revival of *Jane Shore* with one of our highly talented young actresses in the name part might be an interesting experiment. The play is well written and well constructed and the characters well drawn. Its sentimentality is not excessive. A hurdle to be surmounted is the heroine's non-recognition of her supposedly dead husband, who acts as her faithful servitor. The play starts after Jane's royal lover's death:

> Too many giddy foolish hours are gone,
> And in fantastic measures danced away,

as the repentant concubine puts it. Her desire to lead a pious, forgotten life is obstructed by the attentions of Lord Hastings, whose ' tough, impracticable heart ' was only lately ' governed

by a dainty-fingered girl ', the highborn Alicia. He presses his
suit on Jane by brute force and she has to be rescued by her
new servant, who improbably enough is her unrecognized,
deceived husband. He fights the ravisher and disarms him.
With democratic sentiments in advance of his age, the servant
spares the peer:

> Wear your sword again and know a lord
> Opposed against a man, is but a man.

He is arranging for Jane to take refuge in a cottage with ' a
little garden and a limpid brook ', but his plans are thwarted
by Hastings, who has him arrested. Meanwhile Alicia,
Hastings's abandoned mistress, plans her revenge on both
Hastings and her friend Jane, betraying them both to the vengeance of the hunchback Gloucester, Regent of the kingdom.
Hastings declares his loyalty to the infant princes; Gloucester
in vain tries to force Jane to subvert it:

> Go to your Lord, your paramour, begone!
> Lisp in his ear, hang wanton on his neck
> And play your monkey gambols o'er him.
> You know my purpose, look that you pursue it
> And make him yield obedience to my will.
> Do it or woe upon thy harlot's head.

Jane persists in her devotion to the orphan son of her late king
and lover and is driven out to a protracted death:

> Go some of you and turn this strumpet forth.
> Spurn her into the street, and let her perish
> And rot upon a dunghill. Through the city
> See it proclaimed that none on pain of death
> Presume to give her comfort, food or harbour. . . .

Hastings goes to the scaffold charged with high treason.
The final act depicts Jane's Calvary:

> On either side of her marched an ill-looked priest
> Who with severe, with horrid, haggard eyes,
> Did ever and anon by turns upbraid her
> And thunder in her trembling ear damnation.
> Around her, numberless, the rabble flowed
> Shouldering each other, crowding for a view,
> Gaping and gazing, taunting and reviling. . . .

Jane, her hair loose on her shoulders, begs admission at
Alicia's door; but Alicia, crazed by the shock of Hastings's
execution, drives her former friend away:

> Thou hast undone me – murder, oh! my Hastings!
> See his pale bloody head shoots glaring by me.
> Give him me back again, thou soft deluder,
> Thou beauteous witch. . . .

The starving Jane sinks to the ground, where she is found by
her husband. Revealing his identity, he tries to give her food,
but is hurried off by the authorities for disregarding Gloucester's
order. Before he goes, he freely offers his dying wife forgiveness:

> Then all is well [she murmurs] and I shall sleep in peace.
> 'Tis very dark . . . and I have lost you now. . . .

★   ★   ★

Rowe wrote the part of Jane for Mrs Oldfield with Wilks in
mind for the aristocratic Hastings. But when the company
gathered to cast the play, Anne, usually so amenable, declared
that if Booth did not play Hastings, and Wilks the forgiving
husband, she would insist on playing Alicia in place of Mrs
Porter. The author wisely gave in to the intuition of his star,
but it is noteworthy that when illness caused Booth to retire
from the stage, Wilks took over his part. The rôle of the villain
Gloucester fell to Cibber.

The epilogue, addressed to all virtuous wives ' who lead with
horrid husbands decent lives ', was, it is hardly necessary to
say, spoken by Mrs Oldfield, whose silver accents can be caught
echoing down the centuries:

> What if our neighbours have some little failing
> Must we need fall to damning and to railing?
> And since she's dearly paid the sinful score
> Be kind at last and pity poor Jane Shore.

The play scored a huge success and was acted well on into
the nineteenth century. Its sixteenth successive night Anne took
for her benefit.

★   ★   ★

Lady Jane Grey never achieved the same furore, though it ran
ten nights on first production. It saw the light in the year of the

last attempt by the Chevalier de St George to regain the throne
of his fathers. Rowe pulled out all the stops of anti-Jacobite
and anti-papist emotion. Lady Jane, the Protestant pretender
to Bloody Mary's throne, is adjured to save her country from
the horrors Roman Catholicism will bring:

> Behold we stand upon the brink of ruin,
> And only thou canst save us. Persecution,
> That fiend of Rome and Hell, prepares her tortures.
> See where she comes in Mary's priestly train. . . .
> All the mourning year
> Our towns shall glow with unextinguished fires,
> Our youth on racks shall stretch their crackling bones,
> Matrons and husbands with their new-born infants
> Shall burn promiscuous. . . .

Fortunately there are other *motifs* in the play. Lady Jane's
two suitors who vie with each other in nobility of gesture, the
heroine's gentle magnanimity, the implacable heart of Bishop
Gardner (another of Cibber's villainous rôles), all help to keep
the play alive. The end comes when Mrs Oldfield, against the
background of a black-hung scaffold surrounded by guards and
executioners, has a prophetic vision of the first two monarchs
of the Hanoverian line:

> My blood be where it falls; let the Earth hide it
> And may it never rise or call for vengeance.   ·
> Thou gracious Heaven . . .
> Raise up a monarch of the Royal blood
> Brave, pious, equitable, wise and good;
> In thy due season let the hero come
> To save thy altars from the rage of Rome. . . .
> And when he fails, oh! may he leave a son
> With equal virtues to adorn his throne!

As may be expected, the Jacobite element did not take this
without protest. A pamphlet entitled *Remarks on the Tragedy of
the Lady Jane Grey in a letter to Mr Rowe* accuses him of making
the horror of his recent *Jane Shore* still more horrid. The writer
purports to have sat in the Pit next to a grave, attentive old
gentleman. Enquiring of him what the drift of the tragedy
might be, the grave, attentive old gentleman replied that he

believed there was no design in it but to make amends to Mrs Oldfield. Rowe had put her in scandalous circumstances last winter, making her do penance for adultery. Now he had given her as virtuous and sanctified a character as his imagination could provide.

Rowe anticipated criticism for plagiarism. There already existed a play by Banks about the same heroine. It was also generally supposed that Edmund Smith, author of *Phædra and Hippolitus*, had left a draft of a play on the subject. Rowe obtained access to his papers and,

to say the truth, I was a good deal surprised and disappointed at the sight of them. I found the quantity of about two quires of paper written over in odd pieces, blotted, interlined and confused. What was contained in them in general, was loose hints of sentiments and short obscure sketches of scenes. In truth his hints were so short and dark, (many of them marked even in short-hand,) that they were of little use or service to me.

Another play in which Mrs Oldfield acted was inspired by the 1715 rising. This was Cibber's *Non-Juror*. In it she played the coquettish Maria, which part ' she performed to admiration, as she did everything '. The note is struck in a prologue from the pen of the implacable Rowe:

> We mean to souse old Satan and the Pope –
> They've no relations here nor friends we hope!

The play, based on Molière's *Tartuffe* with Cibber as Dr Wolf the Jacobite priest, lives up to that malicious promise, while another character, a Jacobite disguised as a servant, is converted by love of Mrs Oldfield to sound Whig principles. He echoes reminiscence of a youth like Arthur Maynwaring's: ' My father's elder brother ', he says, ' was a gentleman of ancient family in the North. Being himself secretly disaffected to the Government, he gave me in my education the same unhappy prejudices.'

That Cibber anticipated a rough passage for his piece is shown by its epilogue, which must have taken all Anne's courage to speak. Premising that writing a play at all was bold enough, let alone one built on party politics, it was pretended that she had warned the author of the abuse,

. . . . That on his play would fall.
But he, unmoved, cried ' Blood, we'll stand it all!
And if Old England's friends allow 'tis right
We're sure their power will chase the Jacobite
And put their malice, like their troops, to flight ' . . .

The play had a noisy reception and drew a flood of un-
complimentary pamphlets: *The Theatre Royal turned into a
Mountebank's Stage, A Lash for the Laureat, most humbly inscribed to
the unparalleled Mr Rowe on occasion of a late insolent prologue,* and
the rest. But if Cibber made a host of enemies, he collected
one most powerful friend. King George I came to see his play
and sent him round a purse containing two hundred guineas.
That the new monarch could not understand a word of English
possibly impairs the compliment. But it was the beginning of
Court favour that culminated in a laureate's wreath. The bull-
baiting traditions of the audience of that day stimulated interest
in plays like *The Non-Juror*. If the part of the bull was played
by Cibber, his unfailing eye for what his public wanted made
it possible for him accurately to gauge the risk he ran. What the
other actors felt is another question.

Another play in which Mrs Oldfield had the unaccustomed
experience of being hissed, without any political undertone,
was a farcical comedy written in collaboration by Gay, Pope
and Arbuthnot. *Three Hours after Marriage* was sponsored by
Molly Lepell and other ladies of the Court and produced
against the better judgment of the management and partici-
pating cast. A letter ' written by a person of distinction in
London to his friend in the county of Cornwall ' describes the
second night. The storm began immediately after the prologue
and, to the music of cat-calls, the play ' reeled like a ship
tossed in a tempest '. The reception on the first night is elab-
orately described in a rhymed skit called, in honour of the
collaboration, *The Confederates*. This, signed by Joseph Gay, is
really the work of a Captain John Durant Breval.

Gay is represented, reporting to his collaborators on the audience:

Gay   Heroes and Templars here were mixed with wits,
    There bawds and strumpets with a group of cits;
    Ranged in each box were seen the angelic fair,
    Whose footmen have since two been posted there.

Arbuthnot   It promiseth well.
Gay   It did. But mark the end.
        What boots a crowd unless that crowd's your friend?
        The prologue finished, in the Doctor came [Dr Fossile]
        And with him, hand in hand, the intriguing dame
                                [Mrs Oldfield].
        Silent awhile the attentive many sat,
        The men were hushed, the women ceased their chat. . . .
        But soon a murmur in the Pit began
        And thence all round the theatre ran,
        The noise increasing as along it moved,
        Grew loud at last – and to a hiss improved. . . .

The scene shifts to the Greenroom. Mrs Oldfield pours out her heart to Mrs Bicknell, better known as a dancer than an actress:

        Bicknell, it is resolved! Thy arts give o'er
        For from this night I tread the stage no more,
        Hissed and insulted. . . .
        Ill-judging beauties, though of high degree,
        Why did you force this wretched part on me?
        Oh! that I had (with Booth and Wilks combined,)
        Obdurate at first, not changed my mind!

Mrs Bicknell implores Anne to be reasonable. There have been kings and heroes who have retired, sick of worldly pomp, from public life, but never yet an actress. Anne is over-persuaded, ' though used so ill by galleries and pit '; but she vows that if, to please Pope, she appears a second night in his play:

        May Oldfield be the sport of Grub Street bards,
        At ombre always lose and curse the cards.

Her confidante makes a practical suggestion. Surely the three playwrights can raise enough money between them to make it worth going on. Anne interrupts. She has heard Gay's notoriously stumbling footstep outside her door:

        But hark, who is entering here? I'll run away
        For by the clumsy tread it must be Gay!

Left together, Gay offers Mrs Bicknell various inducements

to persevere another night. He promises to write a pastoral play
for her and her friends; Dr Arbuthnot will offer his services as
an accoucheur to Drury Lane free. Mrs Bicknell shakes her
head. Either Mrs Oldfield goes back to the repertory and plays
Jane Shore again or:

> . . . . We must be bought;
> If hissed we are, we'll not be hissed for nought!
> Unless these arts you try, all else will fail
> And guineas, guineas only can prevail!

In the upshot Gay, after trying in vain to raise the money
from Lintot, the publisher, is saved by the renewed contributions of Molly Lepell and two other ladies of the Court.
Pope's unfaltering enmity to Anne becomes more intelligible
if this satire contains the truth.

Another great man of letters who had a less resounding
failure was Addison. After the triumph of *Cato*, he had put his
hand once more into his drawer and brought out a farcical
comedy called *The Drummer*. This time it was Steele he consulted whether to offer it to the Drury Lane management.
Steele advised a few alterations and additions and then to let it go.
Unfortunately the hesitant Addison decided to have it produced
anonymously and so forwent the publicity which his name
would have given to a rather boring affair about a bogus ghost.
A husband supposedly killed at the front, a widow (Mrs Oldfield), courted by a freethinker (Cibber), and a fortune hunter
who dresses up as the ghost of the husband, deserved Mrs
Oldfield's apologetic epilogue:

> My help thus asked, I could not chose but grant it
> And really I thought the play would want it:
> No song, no dance, no music but a drum,
> No smutty thought. . . .

That persistent playwright Mrs Centlivre at last wrote a
good play, *The Wonder*, which amateurs of television have been
able recently to judge for themselves. Mrs Oldfield's performance as Violante won the piece vast popularity and it lingered
on the stage well into the nineteenth century, being even
translated into Polish in 1820. The authoress's *Cruel Gift* was
less happy, although, or because, she had the collaboration of

Nicholas Rowe. The plot was taken from Boccaccio and culminated in the horror-comic situation of Mrs Oldfield, as a
princess of Lombardy, being offered her lover's heart in a
golden cup:

> When one peeped in and hoped for something good
> There was – O God! – a nasty heart and blood. . . .

so she described her feelings in the epilogue.

On the first night the Prince of Wales watched these san-
guinary proceedings from the Royal Box. There is no record
of his reactions, although this experience might excuse his oft-
criticized remark, ' I 'ate bainting and boetry!' In the epilogue
Rowe, now Poet Laureate, did not fail to exploit the pro-
Hanoverian emotions that followed the suppression of the 1715
rising. Mrs Oldfield dropped a deep curtsey to the Royal Box as
she spoke his lines in compliment to the Prince:

> See how his looks his honest heart explain
> And speak the blessings of his future reign;
> In his each feature truth and candour trace,
> And read plain-dealing written in his face!

CHAPTER XX

Such easy gestures, such a graceful port,
So turned and finished for the camp or court.

ADDISON

Enter Brigadier Churchill

WHEN MAYNWARING had been two years in his grave, Anne
moved from her home in New Southampton Street to a house
in the Haymarket, seven doors from the top. Was Southampton
Street too full of memories, or did she simply move with the
fashion that ever extends westward? The new house was tall
and narrow with panelled rooms and gaily painted sash-
windows. She furnished it expensively with embroidered beds
and damask-covered chairs and cabinets displaying china jars.
It was to be her home for twelve years.

For some time she lived there alone. Stories were current
about ' the variety of her amours ', but such ' infamous '
reports arose, said her faithful dresser, from her being more
lovely than the rest of her sex and an object of envy to the
malicious. The stories become circumstantial with a Mr F . . . e,
who had a considerable place in the Customs and who is
claimed to have left a wife and children for her sake. Arthur
Maynwaring had been a Commissioner of Her Majesty's
Customs and on the face of it there is nothing to prevent Anne
having made Mr F . . . e's acquaintance through him. But
Margaret Saunders was very clear. ' As to love affairs, I do
assure you, I know of none but with the fathers of the gentlemen herein mentioned ', that is with Maynwaring and Churchill. Margaret was Anne's dresser for ten years, and before
that had played small parts at Drury Lane since the beginning
of the century. There was little in Anne's private life that was
hidden from her.

If there was any truth in the scandal about Mr F . . . e, it was
not claimed that the affair was of any duration. Anne had little
use for married men, or as a kinder pen put it, 'she never troubled
the repose of any lady's lawful claim'. The scandal-mongers, how-

ever, gave a different reason for the dismissal of the hypothetical
Mr F . . . e: Anne had found a more distinguished lover.

This was not the nebulous Sir Roger Mostings [*sic*], another
of Anne's well-bred admirers. He was a baronet, one of the
handsomest men in England, witty, well-born and rich. He
was passionately in love with Anne, said the gossips, but
received little encouragement.

In 1716 he was in command of the fourth troop of the Life
Guards. The Jacobite lords who had been involved in the rising
the year before were standing their trial. Sir Roger was in-
discreet enough to have been heard wishing them a good
deliverance. He was at dinner when an order came for him to
leave Court. His first thought was that he would have to leave
London and the company of Mrs Oldfield. His grief and love
made him shed tears at table. The baronet's emotion suggested
to him a preposterous remedy. The actress would never go with
him as his mistress. Would she accept the more regular, if
unprecedented, position of a wife?

Anne's answer to this honourable proposal was ' a mortifying
refusal '. She would never give her hand without her heart.
She was improving upon her dismissal of the Duke of Bedford's
less punctilious offer.

Investigation of this edifying tale produces some discouraging
discrepancies. The story is told by the Drury Lane prompter
on the authority of a French author who claimed to have been
present at the momentous meal. Voltaire leaps to the mind.
During his exile in England, Voltaire lodged at the *White Wig*
in Maiden Lane and used regularly to take a sedan chair to the
Theatre Royal. There he borrowed the book of the evening's
play from the prompter and took it to his wonted seat in the
orchestra. Four or five months of this and he could speak and
even write elegant English. He was a fervent admirer of Anne
Oldfield, declaring that, ' She was an incomparable sweet girl.
She reconciled me to the English stage. Her voice, her shape and
all her acting so charmed me that I made haste to learn the
language so that I might understand her.' Indeed, Anne's
diction was so perfect that Voltaire maintained she was the
only actress whom he could follow without effort.

Alas! since he did not come to England until ten years after

the trial of the Jacobite lords, he could not have witnessed the
baronet's grief at the fatal dinner. There is a further difficulty
in accepting the story of the proposal of marriage.

Sir Roger Mostyn, third baronet of Mostyn Hall, Flintshire,
was a contemporary of Anne's. It is likely enough that they
were friends, for he moved in theatrical circles. Farquhar
dedicated his first success *The Constant Couple* to him, ascribing
to him in the normal terms of flattery ' the fire of youth, the
sedateness of a senator, the modern gaiety of a fine English
gentleman and the noble solidity of an ancient Briton '. There
were Jacobite traditions in his family and he may well have
sympathized with the sufferers under the law of high treason.
But the noble solidity of an ancient Briton would have suffered
shipwreck had he ventured to propose marriage to Anne. Since
the early years of the century he had been locked in bands of
holy matrimony to a daughter of the Earl of Nottingham, who
bore him six sons and six daughters.

Unless the baronet was living up to the traditional infamy of his
order, the offer that Anne turned down was, like many another,
uncomplicated by marriage. The only other explanation is that
the unknown French author, or the prompter, confused Sir
Roger with his unmarried, but untitled, younger brother John.

*   *   *

If not Mostyn, who was the distinguished lover that Anne
preferred to all other suitors? She was not getting younger. In
1718 she was thirty-five and Cibber's testimony is that until
her thirty-sixth year her figure was always improving. She could
not overlook the arrival at Drury Lane, from a company of
strolling players, of a potential rival. This was the very beautiful
Mrs Horton, and Barton Booth had given his opinion, which
well-natured friends could be relied on to repeat, that no one
but Mrs Horton was capable of playing Mrs Oldfield's parts.[1]

On the conclusion of peace a certain Colonel Charles
Churchill had come back from the battlefields. ' Our armies
swore terribly in Flanders ', and he is supposed to be the original
of Colonel Ranter in *The Tatler*. That warrior never spoke

[1] Booth's prophecy was fulfilled. After Mrs Oldfield's retirement, Wilks chose Mrs
Horton to play opposite him in *The Way of the World*. Eleven years after Anne's
death, Mrs Horton was in possession of all her parts.

K

without an oath, until he saw Anne Oldfield playing Lady Betty Modish in one of the frequent revivals of the Cibber play:

> Now he never gives an order, but it is ' Pray Tom, do it '. The drawers where he drinks, live in perfect happiness. He asked Will at the *George* the other day, how he did? Where he used to say ' Damn it, it is so,' he now believes there is some mistake, he must confess he is of another opinion.

Alas! in spite of Mrs Oldfield's refining influence, the Colonel's reformation did not last. In his old age he appears in the correspondence of Horace Walpole: ' If you have a mind to know who is adored and has wit, there is old Churchill has as much God-damn-ye wit as ever, except that he has lost two teeth.'

Colonel Churchill came of the most distinguished military family in England. He was the illegitimate son of General Charles Churchill, a younger son of the first Sir Winston and brother of the great Duke of Marlborough. The General, after playing a distinguished part in the Revolution and in all Marlborough's campaigns, was figured prominently in the Press on the morrow of Blenheim. A Colonel Parke brought home a note that the Duke had scrawled with a black lead pencil while on horseback, to inform the Queen that her army had won a great victory. General Churchill in particular, it stated, had distinguished himself. At the head of twelve thousand horse and foot he led a charge against twenty battalions of the enemy defending a system of trenches in the village. He broke through their lines and inflicted heavy losses.

The natural son of this hero was called Charles after his father and inherited all the Churchill courage. After serving with distinction at Oudenarde and Blenheim, the Peace of Utrecht left him temporarily at a loose end. He bought a house in Sherard Street, off Golden Square, Soho, and settled there with the dog he had brought home with him from the war, a French spaniel ' with large chestnut-colour spots and mottled, a short thick head, a thick neck and long coarse hair, two sore spots on his neck and a thick tail of chestnut-colour'. In spite of its eczema, this unattractive pet was very precious to its master.

Colonel Churchill was anything but a recluse. The irregularity of his birth was no obstacle to his practical century and soon he found the place in society that his Churchill blood entitled him to. Lord Hervey, who wrote the famous Memoirs, at first describes him, a trifle patronizingly, as a worthy and good-natured, friendly and honourable man. When he came to know him better, that often cynical observer declared that Charles was ' one of the very few people I love or desire to be loved by – or that I think deserves to be loved '. But the Colonel's best friend was even more prominent, the future Prime Minister, Sir Robert Walpole, whose interests, it was stated, ranged from politics to obscenity and back from obscenity to politics. The vigour of the soldier's language was therefore no obstacle to their friendship. As a practical proof of his esteem Sir Robert presented him with a seat in Parliament for Castle Riding, one of the Walpole pocket boroughs.

At the other end of the social scale must be reckoned his acquaintanceship with the disreputable Colonel Chartres.[1] He had a bet with that notorious card sharper of a hundred guineas, that he could not give up playing hazard. Detected with his elbows on the green cloth, Chartres refused to pay, swearing that he was only punting, not playing. Churchill refused to recognize the distinction and, failing to get satisfaction, carried the case to court where he won a verdict.

This determined character fell deeply in love with Anne Oldfield. He was some seven years the elder. At first his infatuation flourished from afar. On the second night of *Cato*, so concentrated was his attention on the charms of Marcia that after the performance he allowed his beloved spaniel to stray and was obliged to advertise a half-guinea reward and no questions asked. Soon he contrived an introduction to the object of his worship. For four years he proceeded to lay persistent siege to her heart. Anne liked him, admired his courage, was entertained by his wit, flattered by his passion. She had what America calls value sense and she knew what a feather was implanted in her cap by the sedulous courtship of the nephew of the Duke of Marlborough and the bosom friend of the Prime Minister of England. Even the star of Drury Lane could not

[1] At the age of seventy Colonel Chartres had the distinction of being prosecuted for rape by Ann Bond, a maid servant. He was found guilty and sentenced to death. The story has a happy ending with the King granting the Colonel a free pardon and Ann Bond marrying the drawer of a Westminster tavern. The happy pair took an inn in Bloomsbury and set up as its sign – the Head of Colonel Chartres.

ignore that compliment. But never again could she love a man as she had loved Arthur Maynwaring, and Anne, who on the stage played with such realism the flippant, hard-boiled butterfly, cherished secretly in her bosom the commandment not to give her body without her heart.

In the end, after four years' pursuit, she yielded. The Churchill determination, the Churchill charm, the Churchill poetry had its way with her. There was never any question of marriage. Charles Churchill was not the marrying sort. They lived openly together and although passion was buried for Anne in the grave at Chertsey, she was more constant to her Charles than 'millions in the conjugal noose'. Their union, unhallowed by any ceremony, endured happily until the day of her death.

Grub Street imputed ignoble motives to her surrender. She had the good fortune, it declared, to captivate a general officer in the army (for with the lapse of time and the outbreak of war with Spain Charles had been given command of a brigade), who was universally allowed to be a person of as great accomplishment as anyone of his rank. He made it his sole business and delight, he declared, to place her in the same rank of reputation with persons of the best condition.

If this were Anne's ambition, the Brigadier's ever more firmly consolidated position in the highest Whig society made its fulfilment easy. The Prince of Wales had lately installed his Anglophile circle at Leicester House in opposition to his father's more Teutonic establishment at St James's, where sixty-three members of the late Hanoverian household raised their guttural chorus. One of the grooms of the bed-chamber chosen by the Prince was Brigadier Churchill. It was to this exalted sphere that he was allowed to introduce his mistress; and the ex-barmaid, living openly in sin, won all hearts. 'A lady of condition' paid her the tribute of whispering that 'women of the best rank might have borrowed some part of her behaviour, without the least diminution of their dignity'. 'Her natural good sense', said another panegyrist, 'and lively turn of conversation made her way so easy to ladies of the highest rank'. On a summer's morning when the Court was at Windsor or Richmond, she was often to be seen walking arm-in-arm with duchesses and countesses and calling them by their Christian names.

The protection of a nephew, even illegitimate, of the Duke of Marlborough, and Anne's own irreproachable Whig sentiments, smoothed her way. So did her exquisite taste in dress, for there is a freemasonry in fashion which links together women of every degree. But much more was it Anne's own character that won her this ready popularity, as in the much less exclusive society of Edwardian England, the warmth of heart and inescapable charm of the Lancashire mill-hand Gertie Miller carried all before her. A story of a levee at Leicester House instances Anne's superb tact. There was a rumour abroad that she had actually married her Brigadier. The Princess of Wales asked her the direct question. ' So it is said, your Royal Highness,' replied Mrs Oldfield discreetly, ' but we have not owned it yet.' Never could the daughter of a trooper in the Life Guards have administered a hint with greater decorum to a future Queen of England that she should mind her own business.

★   ★   ★

Anne's Brigadier survived their love affair by many years, dying in 1745, a few weeks before his best friend, Walpole. Four lines that commemorate Churchill's relations with the pair of them are well known:

> None led through youth a gayer life than he,
> Cheerful in converse, smart in repartee,
> Sweet was his night and joyful was his day,
> He dined with Walpole and with Oldfield lay.

After Anne had gone, he became something of a bore. Is it unkind to suspect that the seeds were always there and only Anne's gaiety and wit prevented them from being noticed? Hanbury Williams gives a spiteful but convincing picture of the General on a call to the beautiful Duchess of Manchester:

> With old age its vices came along,
> And in narration he's extremely long,
> Exact in circumstance and nice in dates
> On every subject he his tales relates.
> If you name one of Marlborough's ten campaigns,
> He tells you its whole history for your pains,
> And Blenheim's field becomes by the reciting
> As long in telling as it was in fighting.

An example of anecdotage follows that is familiar enough
to-day to sufferers from reminiscences of our later campaigns:

> . . . 'Twas in the year 'ten –
> No, let me recollect, it was not then –
> 'Twas in the year 'eight, I think, for then we lay
> Encamped with all the army near Cambrai.
> Yes, yes, I'm sure I'm right by one event:
> We supped together in Cadogan's tent –
> Palmer, Meredith, Lumley and poor George Grove –
> And merrily the bumpers round we drove;
> To Marlborough's health we drank confounded hard
> For he'd just beat the French at Oudenarde,
> And Lord Cadogan then had got by chance
> The best champagne that ever came from France.
> And 'twas no wonder that it was so good
> For some dragoons had seized it on the road
> And they had heard from those they took it from
> It was designed a present for Vendôme. . . .

The description of the old man, as he bends to compliment the
Duchess on a Staffordshire tea-pot, would have broken Anne's
heart:

> His old desire to please is still expressed,
> His hat's well cocked, his periwig's well-dressed,
> He rolls his stockings still, white gloves he wears
> And in the boxes with the beaux appears.
> His eyes through wrinkled corners cast their rays,
> Still he bows graceful, still soft things he says,
> And still remembering that he once was young,
> He strains his crippled knees and struts along.
> The room he entered smiling, which bespoke
> Some worn-out compliment or threadbare joke,
> For, not perceiving loss of parts, he yet
> Grasps at the shade of his departed wit.

The glimpse that Horace Walpole caught of the old gentleman wearing ' a gouty shoe ' and practising steps before a
mirror to a tune in fashion after the Battle of Oudenarde,
supports this malicious picture.

An even less attractive description was written under a

portrait of the General ' at Van Lowe's by a Lady of Quality ':

> Still hovering round the fair at fifty-four,
> Unfit to love, unable to give o'er,
> A flesh-fly that just flutters on the wing,
> Awake to buzz but not alive to sting –
> Brisk where he cannot, backward where he can,
> The teasing ghost of the departed man.[1]

At the age of fifty-four Charles Churchill was still commanding a regiment of Dragoons. Nine years later he had retired from the service and was appointed Deputy Ranger of St James's Park. Once again Hanbury Williams pilloried him in a rendering of an Horatian ode. The Deputy Ranger is speaking:

> O Venus, Joy of men and gods,
> Leave for awhile thy blest abodes
> And come and visit my land;
> Propitious, on thy votary smile,
> Quit Paphos and the Cyprian Isle,
> And reign in my Duck Island.
>
> Bring too the Graces to my arms,
> Girls that are prodigal of charms
> Of every favour lavish:
> Melting and yielding let them be
> Consider I am sixty-three
> And that's too old to ravish. . . .

A final stanza which invokes Mercury, messenger of the gods and medicament for erring mortals, is too lurid for modern taste. It is clear that after Anne's death her Charles went sadly to pieces.

---

[1] Such is the version in Add Mss 32096 at the British Museum. Lord Warncliffe's edition of *The Letters and Works of Lady Mary Wortley Montagu* (1837) attributes the lines to her and says they were found in a quarto MS of political songs collected by Lady Mary Finch dated 20 June 1733, later in the possession of Charles Kirkpatrick Sharpe. Moy Thomas's edition gives the lines to David Mallet. In the 1759 edition of that poet's works the verses appear as ' On an Amorous Old Man ' and the age of the dotard is lifted from fifty-four to sixty-four. In the 1805 edition of the same writer, the age is reduced to fifty-four, but six lines of less pungent satire introduce the verses. To the present writer they have the authentic venom of Lady Mary's pen.

CHAPTER XXI

Nor will any wise man easily presume to say: ' Had I been in
Savage's condition, I should have lived – or written – better
than Savage.'

S. JOHNSON

Son of Sorrow

IN THE WINTER of 1720 Anne was absent from the stage.
The newspapers reported her dangerously ill, one of them went
so far as to announce her death. As her son Charles was stated
to be about nine in 1730 and was admitted in that year to
Westminster School at that age, there can be no doubt that
Anne's illness was a difficult *accouchement*. As her last baby
Arthur had been born fifteen years earlier and as Anne had
reached the age of thirty-seven, it is not surprising that she had
a bad time. But little Charles throve and eventually lived to
be ninety-two. Theatrical history relates a story of his latter
days.

Five years before Charles's death in 1812, an actor called
Kelly visited Elizabeth Pope, Mrs Siddons's rival, in Lincoln's
Inn Fields and saw a portrait of Anne Oldfield, three-quarters
as large as life, hanging in her drawing-room. ' See what a fine,
marked, tragic brow she has,' said the old actress. ' I myself
believe she was a very good woman ', she added a trifle in-
consequently. Michael Kelly peered into the picture: ' And
who is the little child upon whose head her right hand rests? '
he enquired without much tact. ' Did you never see a very old
man walking about town ', returned Mrs Pope, ' named
General Churchill? '

This third General Charles Churchill had married Anna
Maria, natural daughter of his father's best friend, Sir Robert
Walpole. They had a daughter called Mary who married in
1777 Charles, 1st Earl of Cadogan. Her daughters, Emily and
Charlotte, married respectively the Honourable and Reverend
Gerald Wellesley, Chaplain to Queen Victoria, and Henry
Wellesley, brother of the Duke of Wellington. Henry's son, Lord

SON OF SORROW   153

Cowley, Ambassador in Paris, who handled the Crimean negotiations, was therefore Anne Oldfield's great-great-grandson.
His mother Charlotte Wellesley was spectacularly divorced and
was remarried to the Marquis of Anglesey. Her sons by this
second marriage were Lord Alfred Paget, general in Queen
Victoria's army and her chief equerry, and Lord Clarence
Paget, who commanded her fleet in the Mediterranean. They,
too, were Anne Oldfield's great-great-grandsons.

Returning to her son Charles and his wife Anna Maria
Walpole, there was a daughter Sophia, who married in 1781
Horatio Walpole, afterwards second Earl of Orford. Their
descendant, Lady Dorothy Neville, used to boast of being Anne
Oldfield's great-great-granddaughter. The blood of the one-
time barmaid of the *Mitre* is well distributed among the once
ruling classes of England. As the novelist Hugh Walpole was
Lady Dorothy's nephew, a share of it may also be claimed for
its literary gentlemen.

                ★   ★   ★

Young Charles was born with a silver spoon in his mouth. His
father was a rich man and his mother was earning good money.
She was a good manager, too. She had signed a deed in May
1718, which was witnessed by Margaret Saunders, authorizing
Michael Acton of Old Jewry to sell a thousand pounds of her
stock ' in the Company of Merchants trading to the South Seas
and other parts of America and for encouraging the fishery....'
This was well before the collapse of the South Sea Bubble. A
later deed dated September 1723, witnessed by Brigadier
Churchill, gives a power of attorney to sell another fifteen
hundred pounds stock in the same company. By then the
collapse had come and now she was saving what was possible
from the wreck. No doubt the Brigadier's intimacy with Sir
Robert Walpole, one of the few public figures who came
creditably out of the scandals of the Bubble, enabled him to
give good counsel. And Anne was always ready to take advice.
Her lover's position at Court also indirectly helped her finances.
His finger may be seen in an order the Lord Chamberlain
issued to the managers of Drury Lane:

Whereas I have thought fit, for the better regulation and government of His Majesty's theatre in Drury Lane, to require you to take
care that no benefit might be allowed for the future to any actor
before Mrs Oldfield's and Mrs Porter's benefit night . . .'

Apart from the prestige involved, the earlier in the season a
benefit was given, the larger the receipts.

*   *   *

Before the birth of her second son, Anne had played several
important parts that were new to her. She acted Laetitia in
Congreve's *Old Bachelor*, she took Mrs Barry's part of Arpasia
in Rowe's *Tamerlane*, she played Indiana in Dryden's *Aurungzebe*,
she succeeded Mrs Bracegirdle as Millamant in Congreve's
Way of the World and, for a contrast, she starred as the Cleopatra
of Dryden's *All for Love*.

As Millamant, the critics exclaimed in delight at her fine
figure, attractive manner and harmonious voice. In elegance of
dress, she excelled all her successors except Mrs Abington.

Of Anne's Cleopatra the aged Macklin reported that when
Booth, playing Antony, met Mrs Oldfield in the second act
' their dignity and deportment commanded the applause of the
most judicious critics '. When Antony says,

> You promised me your silence and you break it,
> 'Ere I have scarce begun,

his majesty could only be matched by Cleopatra's respect. In
Shakespeare's phrase, concludes the veteran, ' her bendings
were adornings '. The prompter Chetwood is even more
ecstatic: ' What majestical dignity in Cleopatra! Such a finished
figure on the stage was never yet seen. Her excellent clear voice
of passion, her piercing, flaming eye used to make me shrink
with awe.'

The revival was acted six nights to crowded audiences. The
cast included Mrs Porter as Octavia, Cibber as Alexis and
Wilks as Dolabella. New costumes and sets cost the management six hundred pounds.

Of all her parts, her Cleopatra was preferred by an out-at-
elbows poet who saw her nightly from the Pit:

So bright she shone in every different part
She gained despotic empire o'er the heart;
Knew how each various motion to control,
Soothe every passion and subdue the soul;
As she, or gay or sorrowful, appears,
She claims our mirth or triumphs in our tears.
When Cleopatra's fire she chose to wear
We saw the monarch's mien, the beauty's air.
Charmed with the sight her cause we all approve
And like her lover give up all for love,
Antony's fate, instead of Cæsar's, choose
And wish for her we had a world to lose.

Through his frigid couplets Richard Savage sounds half in
love with his heroine. He had recently made her acquaintance.
Wilks and Steele, who helped him secure a production for his
first play *Love in a Veil*, had introduced him.

Savage was a man of considerable talent whose life was
soured by the belief that he was the unacknowledged bastard of
the Countess of Macclesfield and Lord Rivers. Lady Macclesfield after her divorce became Mrs Anne Brett, the rival of
Jane Rogers for Robert Wilks's wandering affections and the
inspiration of the scarf scene in Cibber's *Careless Husband*. The
scandalmongers said she began her career of gallantry with a
young aristocrat who was also her nephew. She had a beautiful
figure, ' clean-limbed and well-shaped ', but a face ' formed to
excite aversion and not love '. Her lovers described her as one
of the handsomest women – from the chin downward. Lord
Rivers must have kept his eyes downcast. He had two children
by her, a girl who died and the boy Richard, who disappeared
into a maze of baby farming. From these obscurities emerges
a young poet with a reasonably good play in his pocket and an
undoubted chip on his shoulder.

At Drury Lane, where for several years he never missed a
night, he charmed them all into believing his claim to noble
birth and his stories of his inexorable mother. ' That odd being
Richard Savage, son of the late Earl of Rivers ', is the way the
treasurer of the theatre describes him; or again, ' that very
remarkable person Richard Savage, son to the late Earl of
Rivers, with whom I was then intimately acquainted '. Aaron

Hill, playwright, espoused his cause in print. Steele wanted to marry him to his own illegitimate daughter. Wilks went out of his way to plead on his behalf with the formidable Mrs Brett. She kept her one-time lover waiting an hour and eventually promised to finance the penniless poet to the extent of two hundred pounds, fifty of which she actually produced. Anne herself was so pleased with the young man's conversation and touched by his misfortunes that she allowed him a regular pension of fifty pounds, which was paid every year as long as she lived.

That at least is the story believed by Dr Johnson, who was Savage's intimate friend. Theophilus Cibber, Colley's son, who was to act in one of Savage's plays and incurred his all too easy enmity, tells a different tale:

> She so much disliked the man and disapproved his conduct that she never admitted him to her conversation nor suffered him to enter her house. She indeed often relieved him with such donations as spoke her generous disposition. But this was at the solicitation of friends who frequently set his calamities before her in the most piteous light.

The difference in the two accounts centres on how much Anne liked the ' odd being '. Savage, on his nocturnal rambles with Samuel Johnson, would not minimize his friendship with a distinguished actress. Johnson is careful to stress that Savage never saw her alone or in any other place than behind the scenes. The question of sentiment did not arise. But Savage, when he was not busy exploiting his friends or making fresh enemies, could radiate great charm and Anne succumbed to this. Her simple respect for letters could never resist an appeal from any educated beggar. Savage was desperately poor and unhappy. Anne's kind heart responded generously. Moreover, as the mother of two illegitimate sons, she felt a ready sympathy with his bastardy. Lord Rivers, Savage's supposed father, had died of an ' ulcer in the guts ' at Bath in 1712. He left nothing to Savage but, said Charles Macklin, bequeathed Anne Oldfield an eccentric legacy of five hundred pounds. She felt it was her duty to right a wrong with an annual allowance which soon exhausted the capital.

There was never any question of Anne appearing in *Love in a Veil*. It was at the end of the season when it came on, acted by the Drury Lane summer company of younger players under the direction of Mills. Nor did she feel attracted by Savage's more ambitious effort written in his heart's blood, a tragedy on the subject of the murder of Sir Thomas Overbury.

Aaron Hill planned to open a new theatre in the Haymarket and promised to produce his friend's play there. But nothing came of the project. *Overbury* was finally put on for the first night of the Drury Lane summer season of 1723 in very hot weather, with Theophilus Cibber to play the Earl of Somerset, a little-known actress the Countess, and Savage himself, greatly daring, Sir Thomas. It lasted but three nights and next month the unlucky author was reduced to playing a small part in a version of *Henry VI*. But, admits his friend Samuel Johnson, the theatre was a province for which nature had not designed Savage: ' Neither his voice, look nor gesture were such as were expected on the stage.' His *Overbury* was published and the preface contained ' a very liberal encomium on the blooming excellencies of Mr Theophilus Cibber, which Mr Savage could not in the latter part of his life see his friends about to read, without snatching the play out of their hands '.

A few years later the ' son of sorrow ' turned to Mrs Oldfield for assistance more vital even than his annual fifty pounds. Involved in a brawl in a Charing Cross brothel, he had drawn his sword, he asserted in self-defence, and killed his man. He had the misfortune to come up before a hanging judge. What might well have been found manslaughter was brought in as murder and awarded a sentence of death.

As he awaited his doom in Newgate, loaded with irons weighing fifty pounds, he wrote two letters: one for his mother, begging her to come to him, and one to be handed to Wilks. This ended:

As to death, I am easy and dare meet it like a man. All that touches me is the concern of my friends and a reconciliation with my mother. I cannot express the agony I felt when I wrote that letter to her. If you can find any decent excuse for showing it to Mrs Oldfield, do, for I would have my friends and that admirable lady in particular, be satisfied I have done my duty. . . .

Mrs Brett proved obdurate – or worse. She even protested against mercy being shown. Anne Oldfield's heart was made of different material. She won an interview with Sir Robert Walpole. The youth and misfortunes of the victim, sentenced to suffer the extreme penalty, were powerful arguments; his talent, his unfair trial, the lack of premeditation. Sir Robert promised to do his best. The influence of Lady Hertford, patroness of literature, contributed to the poet's salvation and he was released with a free pardon, after he had already ordered a suit of clothes for the scaffold.

But Richard Savage's path lay ever downwards. It may conveniently be followed in Johnson's famous Life. Two of the Doctor's allusions to Anne's bounty catch the eye. The Queen gave the starving poet a banknote for fifty pounds in payment for an Ode celebrating her birthday, with permission to write one every year.

Mrs Oldfield [says Johnson] had formerly given him the same allowance with much more heroic intention. She had no other view than to enable him to prosecute his studies and to set him above the want of assistance, and was contented with doing good without stipulating for encomiums.

When, at the end of his miserable life, Savage was forced to leave the capital and retire to Wales, a subscription for him was raised by his friends. It did not amount to fifty pounds a year, of which Alexander Pope contributed twenty. To quote Johnson again:

Such was the generosity of mankind, that what had been done by a player without solicitation, could not now be effected by application and interest; and Savage had a great number to court and obey for a pension less than that which Mrs Oldfield paid him without exacting any servilities.

Johnson thought little of Anne's morals, but an admiring gratitude for her generosity to his friend lingered long in his memory.

CHAPTER XXII

I saw Hamlet Prince of Denmark played, but now the old
plays begin to disgust this refined age.

JOHN EVELYN

Anne Plays Shakespeare

AS MIGHT BE expected, the inflation and deflation of the
South Sea Bubble affected the theatre, and Anne in particular.
She made her successful investments, though the Press reported
even more sensational profits by Mrs Barbier, the singer. She
realized five thousand pounds from South Sea Stock and did
what Anne would sooner have died than do – retired from the
stage.

Colley Cibber, his eyes ever open to topical opportunity,
exploited the boom in his comedy *The Refusal*, which opened
in February 1721 with Mrs Oldfield in the lead. For the plot
Cibber owed something to Molière's *Les Femmes Savantes*: 'the
frippery of crucified Molière' was how Pope phrased it. Anne's
rôle of a prudish blue-stocking cannot have been congenial.
Nor can the reception of the play have pleased her. Cibber was
reaping the whirlwind sown by his anti-Jacobite *Non-Juror* and
his enemies ' began to hiss it before they had heard it '. The
uproar began the moment Cibber stepped forward to speak the
prologue and lasted the whole of the six nights the play ran.
So Cibber's topical allusion was drowned, when the issuer of
South Sea Stock certificates reaches the name of a famous low
comedian:

O here! William Penkethman one thousand – what! give a
thousand pounds to a player? Why, 'tis enough to turn his brain.
We shall have him grow proud and quit the stage! No, no, keep
him poor. . . .

The next year saw Anne as Mrs Watchit in Susan Centlivre's
last play *The Artifice*. The old names were beginning to drop
out. Rowe was dead and with him the prospect of any more
sure-fire tragic rôles. Now Mrs Centlivre's long series of

comedies of intrigue reached its finish. But a more notable dramatist came back to the stage he had deserted. After more than seventeen years of theatrical silence, Richard Steele returned from politics, journalism and theatrical management to his first love. His come-back, *The Conscious Lovers*, has been described as his finest play.

At least it is the finest flower of sentimental comedy. Based for its situation on a play by Terence (and the tedium of old Roman comedy is recognized by any honest student), its avowed intention was, in Steele's own words, ' the contemplation of distress [which] softens the heart of man and makes the heart better. It extinguishes the seeds of envy and ill will, corrects the pride of prosperity and beats down all that fierceness and insolence which are apt to get into the minds of the daring and fortunate.' A laudable ambition, but doubtfully, as Dennis pointed out, the business of comedy.

The plot is absurd: long-lost fathers and missing daughters, suitors disguised as lawyers or guardians. But Steele was not interested in the plot and in any case Cibber may have suggested it. What interested Steele was social problems: the evil of duelling, the evil of marrying for money, the evil of a married man keeping a mistress, the evil of snobbery. Though to-day little survives but long-winded moralizing, Steele certainly succeeded in interesting and moving the audience of his time.

After his habit, he successfully mobilized the forces of publicity, advertising *The Conscious Lovers* as ' probably the best modern play that has been produced '. New sets were painted, realistic scenes of Charing Cross and the Mall. Anne, the super-innocent heroine, was given magnificent new costumes. The result was sensational. The play ran eighteen successive nights and made the management an unprecedented profit of £2,546 3s 6d, of which six hundred pounds disappeared into Sir Richard's bottomless pocket, together with five hundred guineas that the dedication to George I elicited. Sir Richard expressed himself charmed with all the actors, except Griffin, who played the one unsympathetic part in the piece. In his preface to the printed play he complimented the cast on excelling ' according to the dignity and difficulty of the character they represented '. He reminded his reader that a play is meant to be seen and is bereft of half its effect without the benefit of the acting, urging his readers to go and see for themselves, an advantage which the armchair critic of to-day must forgo.

Anne, as Indiana, won the compliment of tears from Brigadier Churchill as he sat in his box; ' I warrant he'll fight never the worse for that ', said Bob Wilks with the sentimentality the occasion seemed to exact. The General's emotion made the author pride himself that he had improved the technique of comedy by introducing ' a joy too exquisite for laughter '.

Anne, in the epilogue, was supposed to congratulate herself on having at last been given a natural part, instead of the stock artificialities that usually fell to her lot:

> I now can look, I now can move at ease
> Nor need I torture these poor limbs to please,
> Nor with the hand or foot attempt surprise,
> Nor wrest my features nor fatigue my eyes.
> Bless me! what freakish gambols have I played!
> What motions tried and wanton looks betrayed!
> Out of pure kindness all, to over-rule
> The threatened hiss and screen some scribbling fool.
> With more respect I'm entertained to-night,
> Our author thinks I can with ease delight.
> My artless looks with modest graces arm –
> He says I need but to appear and charm.

Fielding's Parson Adams claimed that this was the only play fit for a Christian to see. ' Indeed,' he concludes, ' it contains some things almost solemn enough for a sermon.' And there it may be fair to leave *The Conscious Lovers*.

Anne's next venture was off her beaten track. She broke, for her, new ground by appearing in what passed in her day for Shakespeare.

At the beginning of the seventeen hundreds the plays of Shakespeare were far from unpopular. Rich's account book, besides showing the takings of his own theatre, gives lists of the plays acted at Drury Lane for the triumvirate. These record for the season 1724/5 four performances each of *Hamlet* and *Julius Cæsar*, three of *Othello*, *Timon* and *The Tempest*, and two of *Henry IV*, *Henry V*, *Henry VIII*, *King Lear* and *Macbeth*.

L

The difference in approach from our own was not perhaps so great. Whereas to-day the plays are butchered to make a producer's holiday, in Anne's time they were distorted to suit the pleasure of an adapter. To-day every word, however turgid, written by the author or by one of his manager's hacks, is carefully preserved, while the utmost liberty in presentation and interpretation is encouraged.

When Mrs Oldfield ventured on the part of Queen Margaret in Shakespeare's *Henry VI, Part 2*, she did it through the medium of an adaptation by Ambrose Philips called *Humfrey Duke of Gloucester*. Had she been tempted by the part of Rosalind she could, in place of *As You Like It*, have selected Charles Johnson's *Love in a Forest*; if Beatrice, she could shortly have found *Much Ado* brought up to date by James Miller as *The Universal Passion*. D'Urfey had 'improved' *Cymbeline* into *The Injur'd Princess*. Cibber was to point the Protestant moral of *King John* in his *Papal Tyranny in the Reign of King John* (Cibber played this lead when he had just lost his teeth. He was inaudible but the audience was much entertained by his ' attitudes and conduct '). Aaron Hill converted *Julius Cæsar* into *Roman Revenge*, and Gildon *Measure for Measure* into *Beauty the Best Advocate*. *The Tempest* and *Macbeth* were presented as operas, the latter with a chorus of witches, and *Lear* was given a happy ending.

> Rough was the Language, unadorned the Stage
> And mean his Hero's Dress in Shakespeare's Age:

such was the conviction of the early eighteenth century, and the habit of employing men experienced in stage authorship to correct these weaknesses was possibly preferable to the subsequent practice of leaving it to the actor, however eminent:

> Mr Quin had during the course of his acting, from his judgement in the English language and knowledge of the history of Great Britain, corrected many mistakes which our immortal bard Shakespeare, by oversight or the volatileness of his genius, suffered to creep into his words. He also changed many obsolete phrases . . .

The liberties which Garrick afterwards took, and Irving, are notorious.

On 12 March 1716 Mrs Oldfield spoke an epilogue, no

doubt a facetious one designed to remove any feelings of gloom, to *Hamlet*. This may strike the student of the theatre as inexpedient, as does the singing and dancing which ' a young lady equally famous for her beauty, her spirit and her virtue, to the glory of her sex and the shame of ours ' got omitted from a performance of *Julius Cæsar*. The age did not take the works of William Shakespeare with quite that solemnity that this century, secure in the discovery that entertainment tax need not be paid on his plays, is apt to manifest.

In Philips's version of *Henry VI*, which Anne acted nine times, only some thirty lines were Shakespeare's. Divided into fifty-three scenes, the piece neglects the unities with a contempt equal to its great original's. Anne played Queen Margaret, Booth Humfrey, Duke of Gloucester, and a small part was given to Eli (Elizabeth?) Oldfield, of whom all further trace is lost.

Anne's success spurred her to attempt a better-known Shakespearean part, Princess Katherine in *Henry V*, as seen through the eyes of the versatile Aaron Hill. Rewriting Shakespeare was only a part-time employment of that tall, ' genteelly-made ' young man with the dark-blue eyes, brown hair and oval face: ' his poetical pieces were the product of leisure hours, when he relaxed his thoughts from the various study of history, geography, physic, commerce etc. '

In other leisure hours he formed companies for the extraction of oil from beech-mast and for the manufacture of potash. He owned and largely wrote a newspaper which had carried an account of the misfortunes of Richard Savage. He bought a tract of land in America which eventually became the State of Georgia. Then ' in 1723 Mr Hill brought his tragedy of Henry V upon the stage at Drury Lane, which play varies much from Shakespeare's, but where the characters have similitude, those parts may be said to be an improvement on the great Shakespeare ', as his loyal editor stoutly asserts. By sweeping away all the comedy (and who would not be quit of the humours of Ancient Pistol?) Hill made room for a sub-plot round a character he called Harriet, daughter of Lord Scrope. Before the play starts, she has been the forsaken mistress of Henry, ' this traitor king, this ravisher of women ', as she calls him when she hears of his plan to marry the French princess. For disguised as Owen

Tudor, Henry has travelled to the French Court, where he has seen, and fallen in love with, Katherine.

Harriet, in male dress, penetrates to the Dauphin's camp to warn Katherine (Mrs Oldfield) of Henry's matrimonial intentions, which excite the Princess's indignation:

> Love is a flame too bright, too clear, to burn
> As interest bids it. . . .

Harriet avows the plot headed by her father, Lord Scrope, to assassinate Henry, excusing it in the name of ' the countless crowds of beauties he has ruined '.

Katherine attends a parley between the French and English kings, at which Henry's speech about ceremony is transferred to the competent hands of Mrs Oldfield. To her delight and astonishment she recognizes in the King of England her former visitor:

> O, my high beating heart! 'Tis Tudor's voice.

She sends a page to warn him of the murder plot; otherwise the parley has served no useful purpose:

Henry	No more! When next we meet our swords shall argue.
French Herald	Why then 'tis war.
Dauphin	'Tis glory and revenge.

Katherine secures a safe conduct to pass through the armies to Agincourt Castle.

Henry confronts Harriet with the discovery of her plot: ' 'Tis true, fair murderess, I have greatly wronged thee ', and at the end of the duologue Harriet stabs herself:

> Harriet, the injured Harriet, dies,
> Oh! see the fatal fruits of guilty love!

Katherine, on her way to Agincourt Castle, begs Henry to call off the battle in quittance for the service she has just rendered him:

Katherine	Accept the terms my father lately offered
	And pay me back the debt you owe my care.
Henry	That were to prove unworthy your regard.

But while they talk, the Dauphin orders the attack and the Princess is escorted to the castle.

For a time, with the scene in the Dauphin's camp and the St Crispin's Day speech in the English lines, the play joins up with Shakespeare's. Then at the sound of a charge heralded by drums and trumpets, the Genius of England rises through a trap door and sings an Ode which begins: ' Earth of Albion open wide and give thy rising Genius way! ' and ends with the rout of ' the fainting Gauls '.

More authentic Shakespeare follows and all ends happily with the marriage in prospect and the calling off of the pursuit in lines of unparalleled banality:

Katherine	Oh! noble Henry! Spite of that esteem
	Thy glittering virtues strike my wond'ring soul with,
	Some sighs must be allowed to sad reflection,
	How dear our promised joys have cost our country.
Henry	The tender woe becomes thy gentle nature.
	Uncle of Exeter, send word to stop
	Pursuit and stay the hand of desolation:
	We must not waste a country we have won . . .

Aaron Hill, who was a man of substance, spent two hundred pounds out of his own pocket having ' most great and elegant ' scenery painted for this nonsense, which delighted, however, several foreign ambassadors. Booth acted Henry and Wilks the Dauphin. Booth did some canvassing and visited many ' men of figure ' to extol the beauties of the play, which he declared well worthy of Shakespeare. He asked an intermediary to tell Princess Caroline about it. She promised to order a command performance after the Christmas holidays, but conveniently forgot. King George and the Princess of Wales, however, attended Mrs Oldfield's next benefit, Beaumont and Fletcher's *Rule a Wife and Have a Wife*.

CHAPTER XXIII

While Autumn, nodding o'er the yellow plain
Comes jovial on.

J. THOMSON

Pulchrorum Autumnus Pulcher

THUS ENDED Anne Oldfield's experiments with so-called Shakespeare. Doubtless she felt more at ease in contemporary comedy, which was at least honest, and in the stilted classical tragedy of the day.

Her new play was the piece Gay read to Princess Caroline, falling over her foot-stool and knocking over her screen: ' by the clumsy tread it must be Gay.' This was *The Captives*, in which Wilks and Mrs Porter were King and Queen of Media, and Booth and Mrs Oldfield their prisoners from Persia. Mrs Oldfield, helping her husband to escape hidden under her discarded veil, is left in his place to her fate. The implacable Mrs Porter, who has been making overtures to Barton Booth, demands her execution, but Robert Wilks, saved by Booth from assassination, magnanimously reprieves her and the play ends happily with Mrs Porter's suicide. The critics liked the play and its performers: ' Mr Booth and Mrs Oldfield outdid themselves at that surprise of meeting in prison.' They were provided with good parts by the author and ' well improved ' them. A distinguished spectator came from afar to applaud their performance. On the third night the Ambassador of Morocco sat in the front row of the Royal Box, flanked by the Master of the Revels and the late British Ambassador to his country. Behind the Moor was ranged his retinue. He expressed himself very well pleased with the play, of which he must have understood about as much as George I did of Anne's benefit Beaumont and Fletcher. He wanted to pay for his seat, but the Master of the Revels explained it was unnecessary. Three weeks later the Ambassador revisited the Royal Box with nine of his staff and was prevented with difficulty from giving the box-keeper four guineas.

Cibber had not written a play for three years, but on 9 December 1724 Anne played Cleopatra in his new tragedy, called *Cæsar in Ægypt*, a melodrama based on a play of Fletcher's. ' Ægyptian Cibber ', said the critics, had already written two tragedies which were so bad that they were hissed by schoolboys. His latest effort was ten times worse. Nevertheless, his brother managers agreed to spend seven hundred pounds on new scenery and costumes. The scenic effects featured cardboard swans, which were towed by concealed stage hands along a painted Nile. Mrs Oldfield scored her usual hit in the consolatory epilogue:

> Say, nymphs who've seen this Cleopatra die,
> Were you then cured of love? Or did you say
> ' O Ged, my lord! Would you were Antony!

In spite of the strident hiss which, Fielding remarks, ' welcomed his Cæsar to the Egyptian shore ', Cibber's tragedy lasted six consecutive nights.

There was at this time a great shortage of new plays of any merit. ' Cibber tells me ', wrote Vanbrugh to the bookseller Tonson, ' 'tis not to be conceived how many and how bad plays are brought to them.' In despair the management cast about for old plays that had not been recently acted with parts calculated to exploit Anne's personality. Such were Farquhar's *Twin-Rivals*, which had not seen the stage for twenty years and which provided Anne with the not very exciting part of Aurelia. The play peters out before the end but has some brilliant comedy in the first half with Mrs Mandrake, the midwife-procuress. The revival stood up for three consecutive nights, and a fourth was commanded by the Prince and Princess of Wales.

A more successful revival was Vanbrugh's *Provok'd Wife*. The Court and ' many of the nobility ' demanded this piece. The producer felt that popular taste had changed with the years and that certain revisions by the author were called for, notably in the disguise of a parson adopted by Sir John Brute. ' The character and profession of a fine lady not being so indelibly sacred ', that travesty was substituted.

An altercation occurred when the play came up for casting.

Wilks had set his heart on playing the hero, Constant. It was suggested that there was less action in the part than in those he usually portrayed. ' Here Wilks looked grave.' The love scenes, said somebody, were serious and would suit Booth better. ' Down dropped his brow.' Wilks could not play *every* comedy lead or what would happen, supposing he fell ill? ' Here he pretended to stir the fire.' The part would add nothing to his reputation. His reaction was a flood of obscenity; the management, he saw, was trying to oust him from a play the Court had commanded. ' Very well,' said Cibber, ' you hold the part in your hands. It is a matter of indifference to us whether you take it or leave it.' Wilks threw down the part on the table, crossed his arms and sat knocking his heel on the floor. Booth protested that he did not want to act every night; his state of health would not let him; he was prepared to yield any claim to the part. At this point Mrs Oldfield was observed, tittering behind her fan. Wilks ignored her. In answer to Booth, he said he himself was not as strong as a cart horse and that if Mrs Oldfield would choose somebody else to act opposite her, he would be glad to be excused. This was, as would now be said, passing the buck to Anne. Cibber tried to come to her rescue, explaining that it was a poor compliment to the company to suggest that only one actor could play this very ordinary part. Anne saw that the time had come for her to take a hand. She was an excellent psychologist and knew how to handle jealous men. She rose to her feet and said ' with her usual frankness, " Pooh! you are all a parcel of fools to make such a rout about nothing! ", rightly judging that the person most out of humour would not be the more displeased at her calling us all by that name '. She proceeded to pour balm on Wilks's hurt feelings by expressing the hope that he would forgive what had been said and not refuse to act with her. The part might not be as good as those he was accustomed to play, but she knew that the Court circles which had asked for the play would want to see it acted to the best advantage. She added that it would make an odd story, if it leaked out that there had been any dispute among the managers about casting the part.

Anne's tact had composed the dispute. Wilks got the part, and the other managers made their point that he was not always to get first pick. The heroine of the quarrel played Lady Brute with her usual success and the revival, with new dresses for her to wear, ran seven consecutive nights. It was repeated for her benefit in March.

Anne's most showy part in this series of revivals was Calista in Rowe's *Fair Penitent*, which had originally been played by Mrs Barry. This ' melancholy tale of private woe ' had Rowe's usual excellence of plot and characterization. Calista, who had had a pre-marital affair with Lothario, is the cause of a duel between husband and lover in which the lover is killed. Her outraged father shuts her up with the corpse and offers her a dagger. This last act gave Mrs Oldfield all the scope any tragic actress could wish. ' The room is hung with black. On one side Lothario's body on a bier. On the other a table with a skull and other bones, a book and a lamp on it. Calista is discovered on a couch in black, her hair hanging loose and disordered.' After distant music and a song: ' Hear, you midnight phantoms hear ', she rises:

> 'Tis well, these solemn sounds, this pomp of horror,
> Are fit to feed the frenzy in my soul,
> Here's room for meditation ev'n to madness
> Till the mind burst with thinking. This dull flame
> Sleeps in the socket. Sure this book was left
> To tell me something. For instruction then . . . (*she reads*)
> He teaches holy sorrow and contrition
> And penitence. Is it become an art then?
> A trick that lazy, dull, luxurious gownmen
> Can teach us to do over? (*she throws the book away*)

A story is told of the old days when Mrs Barry played Calista and the dissolute George Powell, Lothario. It was Powell's habit sometimes to let his dresser understudy as the corpse. Forgetting this arrangement, one night needing the man's services, he called him from backstage. The dresser lay mute. ' Come here, sir! ' Still no answer. ' Come here, you son of a whore, or I'll break every bone of your body.' Terrified, the dresser jumped up. His shroud was fastened to the bier. He dragged it with him, upsetting in his course table, lamp, bones, book, skull - and Mrs Barry.

June 1727 saw the death of George I on a visit to his continental dominion. In October his son was crowned. Drury Lane ' invented and adorned a spectacle that for forty days together brought more money to the house than the best play that was ever writ ', says one of its managers proudly. This was a stage Coronation ceremony. With some justification it was tacked on to the Henry VIII drama of *Virtue Betray'd*, in which Anne played Anne Bullen. It was tacked on, with less relevance, to *Jane Shore*, in which Anne played Jane. It was tacked on to *The Way of the World*, in which Anne played Millamant, with no connection at all.

But however brazenly the box office might rejoice over this *tour de force*, there can be no doubt that the biggest Drury Lane draw of those years was Anne's playing of Lady Townly. In Cibber's re-write of a play that Vanbrugh's death had left unfinished, she scored at the age of forty-five the biggest comedy hit of her career. One enthusiastic critic describes it as the *ne plus ultra* of her art: ' she slid so gracefully into the foibles and displayed so humorously the excesses of a fine woman too sensible of her charms, too confident in her strength and led away by her pleasures. . . .' *The Provok'd Husband* provided her with a part that fitted her like a glove and triumphantly she filled it.

On Vanbrugh's unfinished draft of *The Journey to London* of a country squire and his cheating by a foreign sharper, Cibber grafted the story of the married life of Lady Townly and her lord. His avowed object (it was now the fashion to take a leaf out of Steele's book of morality) was ' to expose and reform the licentious irregularities that too often break in upon the peace and happiness of the married state '. The picture Anne's conversation with her sister-in-law draws of this peace and happiness is not unentertaining:

Lady Townly   Oh! there is no life like it! Why t'other day for example, my lord and I after a pretty cheerful tête-à-tête meal, sat down by the fire-side in an easy, indolent, pick-tooth way for about a quarter of an hour, as if we had not thought of any other's being in the room. At length, stretching himself and yawning, ' My dear,' says he, ' Aw – you came home very late last night? ' ' Twas but just turned of two ', says I. ' I was in bed – aw – by eleven,' says he. ' So you are every night.' ' Well,' says he, ' I am amazed you can sit up so late.' ' How can you be amazed,' says I, ' at a thing that happens so often? ' Upon which we entered into a conversation and, though this is a point has entertained us above fifty times already, we always find so many pretty new things to say upon it, that I believe in my soul it will last as long as we live.

Lady Grace   But pray, don't there, now and then, enter some little witty sort of bitterness?

Lady Townly   Oh! yes! A smart repartee, with a zest of recrimination at the head of it, makes the prettiest sherbet. Ay! Ay! if we did not mix a little of the acid with it, a matrimonial society would be so luscious that nothing but an old liquorish prude would be able to bear it.

Lady Grace   Well, certainly you have the most elegant taste!

Lady Townly   Though to tell you the truth, my dear, I rather think we squeeezd a little too much lemon into it this bout. For it grew so sour at last, that I think I almost told him he was a fool and he talked something oddly of turning me out of doors.

Cibber's Tory enemies did their best to wreck the first night; but the author was either so philosophical or so exhausted that between acts he was discovered asleep in the wings. On top of the cares of authorship he was playing the country squire.

Without Anne's superb performance the verdict on the play would have been ' a dead and damned piece '. Although she was forty-five, in a society where dentists and beauty specialists were primitive, if existent, she rushed upon the stage, recorded one who was present, with the full consciousness of youth, beauty and attraction. She answered all Lord Townly's questions ' with such lively indifference, as to mark the contrast in their way of thought as much as in their manner of speech '. When she came to describe the privileges of a married woman, she repeated her lines ' with a rapidity and *gaité de cœur* that electrified the whole house ':

To begin with in the morning a married woman may have men at her toilet; invite them to dinner; appoint

> them to a party in a stage box at the play; engross the
> conversation there; call 'em by their Christian names;
> talk louder than the players; take a frolicksome supper
> at an India house; crowd to the hazard table; throw a
> familiar levant upon some sharp, lurching man of
> quality and if he demands his money, turn it off with
> a loud laugh and cry you'll owe it to him. . . .

When Wilks, as Lord Townly her husband, met this tirade
with a half-sarcastic, half-admiring ' Prodigious! ', the audience
applied his comment to the actress and shouted and echoed the
word in a burst of frenzied applause.

Still the interruptions to that part of the play which Cibber's
enemies had decided was his, went on, although his subsequent
publication of Vanbrugh's fragment proved their attribution
mistaken. At certain lines in the fourth act, the actors had to
stand silent and still, while the storm raged. At length a final
reconciliation between husband and wife rounded off the tale;
in a lull Anne came forward to speak the epilogue:

> Methinks I hear some powdered critics say,
> ' Damn it! This wife reformed has spoiled the play. . . .'

A man ' of undistinguished appearance ' standing right in
front, next to the orchestra, greeted her words with a loud hiss.
Anne Oldfield stopped; fixed her lovely eyes on him; judged
another pause and let fall the words ' Poor creature! '. Before
her look of mingled scorn and pity, the interrupter subsided
and Anne was left to finish the epilogue in admiring silence:

> You, you then, Ladies, whose unquestioned lives
> Give you the foremost fame of happy wives,
> Protect for its attempt this helpless play
> Nor leave it to the vulgar taste a prey,
> Appear the frequent champions of its cause,
> Direct the crowd and give *yourselves* applause!

She saved the night. The play ran twenty-eight successive
performances and was still grossing one hundred and fifty
pounds when it was taken off. She formed, said the critics, the
centre of appreciation from her looks, her dress, her admirable
performance. All her successors in the part concentrated their

efforts on being well-bred, and gave tame, flat performances. Anne alone ' gave it all the rage of fashion and vivacity '.

In his preface to the published play, the author let his gratitude run away with his pen: ' It is not enough to say ', he wrote, ' that Mrs Oldfield outdid her usual outdoing.' His foes were ever on the look-out for Cibber's solecisms:

> How with less reading than makes felons 'scape,
> Less human genius than God gives an ape. . . .

and the actor-playwright had to apologize to his readers in a later edition:

A most vile jingle [he wrote] I grant it and I owe myself the shame of confessing I have no excuse for it, but that, like a lover in the fullness of his content, by endeavouring to be blindly grateful, I talked nonsense.

It is improbable that Anne, in her triumphant autumn, objected to his nonsense.

CHAPTER XXIV

The seeds of dark disease.

J. THOMSON

Our Lady of Pain

ABOUT A YEAR earlier a sinister entry appeared in Rich's account book:

> Saturday 7th January 1727. Dismissed *The Careless Husband*; because Mrs Oldfield was taken ill.

Often the pain was severe, so bad that, though she went on acting, the tears used to run down her cheeks. But this was the first time that she had had to give in to it and allow the piece to be abandoned. The play must go on. That was the tradition of her profession. She did not know what caused the pain; she did not want to know. She dared not guess and, said her dresser, the natural cheerfulness of her temper made her ward off every attack with the greatest alacrity. But this time, when it came to trying to play Lady Betty Modish, the part in which she had made her first big hit, the part that came most easily to her lips, the part that, long ago, Arthur Maynwaring had taught her, she could not go on. She collapsed.

They put her in her coach and drove her to Lower Grosvenor Street, to Number 59, where she had moved from the Haymarket a year or two before. The quarter was new and its houses were recently completed. She and Charles had chosen Number 59 together and had furnished it in a manner ' most elegant and fashionable '.

The four-poster her servants laid her on was hung with damask silk, so were those chairs which were not covered with chintz or embroidery. Standing on the chimney-piece was a curious French clock, the work of the master Delander. On the walls were pieces of tapestry after Teniers. On the floor lay a carpet ' of the nicest sort '. From the bed she could see her dressing-table. On its surface of flounced and chintzy elegance gleamed the silver of her dressing set. Margaret Saunders was putting away in their cases the jewels she had taken off her mistress's neck and fingers. Anne was fond of jewellery.[1] She had a string of fine large pearls, and a necklace of thirty-seven garnets with a diamond set in each, and another diamond necklace of thirty-four brilliants. Ear-rings suited her. She had five pairs: diamond, emerald, ruby and garnet. Five diamond and brilliant rings set off her slender fingers. Her favourite jewel was a cross of very fine emeralds set with small brilliants. She always wore it and had been painted by Kneller with it round her neck. Besides, she had a garnet cross that dated from humbler days. In another box Margaret arranged the trinkets given her by ambassadors and grandees after her stage triumphs: an enamelled miniature of Louis XIV, another miniature of a nobleman on gold, but she had forgotten his name; two gold snuff boxes, one set with brilliants and rubies; a gold repeating watch and chain, ornamented with brilliants, rubies and lapis lazuli; three more gold watches, one by Hubert and one by Poy; a gold smelling bottle; all tributes paid by admiring wealth, grandeur and nobility. But Anne lay uncaring on her bed and would have given all her treasures to be quit of suffering.

Was this bedroom, she wondered mistily, fated to become her little world, and would she ever see again the rooms she was so proud of? Her library with its pretty collection of books in English and French?[2] Her dining-room with her plate on the sideboard? The other apartments with sconces and branched candlesticks on the walls, lustres hanging from the ceiling; pier glasses between the windows and looking-glasses over the chimneys; Indian chests and cabinets displaying her valuable old china?

She was proud, too, of her pictures. Many of them commemorated her stage triumphs. That portrait of the Earl of Essex, supposed to be a Holbein, was given her after she had played the lead in Banks's *Unhappy Favourite*. She had tried to look like that head of Anne Bullen in his *Vertue Betray'd*, while that group of the Stuarts by a pupil of Van Dyck was a memento of her early hit as Mary Stuart. How honoured she had felt

---

[1] Her jewellery was said to be worth £11,000.
[2] A collection of plays that was said to be hers was bought after her death by Queen Caroline for the large sum then of £120. The newspapers even reported the figure of £200.

when the late King had given her the portrait of himself by
Kneller, so diplomatically kind to the protuberant eyes and
roman nose! To register her Protestant, Whig sympathies she
had hung that head of Bradshaw, the regicide, painted by
Samuel Cooper. Charles had bought her the historical subject
by Sebastian Ricci, the master of Pelegrini, who had visited
England and had executed various commissions here. He had
given her, too, a couple of Dutch seascapes from the brush of
Johann Breughel, and a luscious Venus and Adonis by Luca
Giordano, whom the Neapolitans nicknamed *Fa Presto*, so
speedy was his hand at copying the old masters; religious subjects as well – a Holy Family, supposed to be by Raphael, and
a Madonna with Angels, by Muratti.

Then there were statues. As a set-off against the head of
Bradshaw, she had bought the full-length ivory figure of
Strafford, carved by Grinling Gibbons. She had commissioned
the marble statue of her son, Charles, when he was quite little.
Between a couple of antique vases stood an ivory bas-relief of the
Judgment of Paris, and near it a Venus cast in bronze and a Dog
'curiously performed in marble'. It was Charles's French spaniel
that he had brought back with him from the front. However
loyally she had tried, she had never loved that dog as she had old
Monsieur Adonis, the one Farquhar had given her, who lasted
into Arthur's day. . . . Dear old Monsieur Adonis. . . . The pain
was a little better now. Perhaps she could sleep and stop wonder-
ing whether she would ever see her possessions again?

★   ★   ★

When she was better she went quickly back to work. Rehearsals
had started for a new play which was due to open in three
weeks. She could not indulge herself. Then came her triumph
in *The Provok'd Husband* and she tried to let no one know that
she was not in the rudest of health. While the piece was still
running, she had to engineer the meeting with the Prime
Minister to try and beg off poor Dick Savage from his horrid
fate. That drew on her reserves of energy. Before the run of the
play was over, *The Beggar's Opera* opened at the rival house.
The triumvirate made the biggest mistake of their administra-
tion in missing that piece, but their patience with Gay's succes-

sive failures had become exhausted, and really a Newgate pastoral did not sound box office. So Gay went to Rich, who had the crazy idea of casting the nearly unknown Lavinia Fenton as the delicious Polly Peachum. The Opera opened to one hundred and sixty-four pounds twelve shillings and for the sixty-two nights it ran that season it averaged one hundred and seventy pounds. On the twenty-eighth night the King and Queen and the young Princesses were in the Royal Box. Anne would not have been human if she had not remembered with pleasure that the royal party had been to see her Lady Townly first. She did not appreciate the lines the wits were murmuring:

> While Polly charms the present age
> And Venus' train the Fair commands,
> *Autumnal* Oldfield boils with rage
> And rugged Porter grimly frowns. . . .

Another person who did not congratulate himself on Miss Fenton's furore was Henry Fielding, aged twenty-one. He had had his first play *Love in Several Masques* accepted by Drury Lane and Anne had consented to play the lead: a rich widow whose three suitors evaporate when they hear a false rumour that she has lost her money.

' I believe ', the young dramatist wrote in his preface to the published work, ' few plays have ever adventured into the world under greater disadvantages than this. First, as it succeeded a comedy, which for the continued space of twenty-eight nights received as great and as just applause as were ever bestowed on the English Theatre.' (Cibber's troubled first night had quite passed out of short theatrical memory.) ' And secondly, it is contemporary with an entertainment which engrosses the whole talk and admiration of the town.'

This compliment did not preclude a dig at Gay's masterpiece when Anne in the Fielding play is made to ask, ' Who expects wit in a lover any more than good music in an English opera, or common sense in an Italian one ?'. ' Such was the candour of the audience ', the young author concludes, ' my play was received with greater satisfaction than I should have promised myself from its merit, had it even preceded *The Provok'd Husband* '.

M

Fielding goes on to mention the ' civil and kind behaviour '
of Wilks and Cibber at rehearsals and the merit of their subsequent performance. He commemorates Anne's excellent
judgment in some alterations she suggested at rehearsals for
which, he says, he takes credit in the published text. He
expresses his gratitude to her for being willing to play Lady
Matchless ' though she had contracted a slight indisposition by
her violent fatigue in the part of Lady Townly '. Anne knew
only too well this was no slight indisposition brought on by
overwork. Ready, as always, to help young genius at the start
of its course, she forced herself to endure the labour of rehearsals
and the strain of the first night and the exertion of the play's
brief run. In Anne's ears rang the words of the song that ends
the play:

> Let meaner things be bought or sold,
> But beauty never trucked for gold.

It is only fair that the pen of Henry Fielding should pay her
a compliment which echoes down the dusty corridors of theatre
history, since, as Steele puts it, Apollo is a physician even after
death: ' The ravishing perfections of this lady are so much the
admiration of every eye and every ear that they will remain
fixed in the memory of many when these light scenes shall be
forgotten.'

★　　　★　　　★

A fortnight later the night of Anne's benefit came round. It
was freezing hard but the house was packed and the benches
which had to be put on the stage to make room were enclosed
to keep out draughts. In spite of the weather their Majesties
were present. The play chosen was Vanbrugh's *Relapse*, the
famous Lord Foppington play, in which Mrs Oldfield was
Berenthia. She got through the evening and for her the end of
the season was in sight.

That spring Charles Churchill had to leave her. He was sent
to Paris on a mission, to induce ' Bobbing John ', Earl of Mar,
said the Jacobites, to betray Bishop Atterbury. The Brigadier
was observed at the opera; at the theatre, too, where the
Lecouvreur was still to be seen. He wanted to know if there
was any truth in what Lady Mary Wortley Montagu was

saying, that his mistress was only fit to play the French tragedienne's confidante. There were always people, he decided, to find no merit in their own countrywomen. Churchill was back in England at the end of the first week in June and Anne had need of quiet until the autumn season began. Then on 16 November 1728 she appeared in her old triumph *The Distrest Mother*, and somehow kept going through the long, exacting part. The effort was too great, and two days later the papers were carrying the news that she was very ill at her house in Grosvenor Street. Ten days later she was up again to play in Beaumont and Fletcher's *Wit without Money*, and four nights later in their *Scornful Lady*. For her benefit next March the management (or the Queen, for it was by royal command) mercifully accepted the light part of Leonora in *Sir Courtly Nice*, the play in which Cibber had discovered her potentialities a quarter of a century earlier.

That summer another link with the past was broken and Steele died, partly paralysed, in Wales. On a summer's evening he used to have his servant carry him out of doors to watch the country-folk dancing. To the best performer he gave a pencilled order (for he could still write, though speech was difficult) on the local mercer for a new gown. He had been made Supervisor of the Theatre Royal soon after George I's arrival in England, and after his death the newspapers printed a paragraph stating that his Patent for Drury Lane had been transferred to Mrs Oldfield by command of the Crown. The Lord Chamberlain's papers, however, contain no confirmation of this story. The Court may have mooted the project to make the ailing actress happy without ever giving formal effect to it.

Suspecting that her time was short, she made up her mind to give her public full value in her last season. What that resolution cost her the cold light of statistics can show. Between 11 September 1729 and her final appearance on the stage on 28 April 1730 she played eighty nights and acted in twenty-eight different plays. Two of them were new plays with the inevitable rehearsals and first-night strain. Twice she was too ill to continue and the curtain had to come down on *The Beaux Stratagem* and on *The Careless Husband* again. All her other great parts she gave the public for the last time: Andromache, Jane

Shore, Anne Bullen, Marcia, Calista, Mary Stuart from the
tragedies; from the comedies Millamant, Lætitia, Lady Townly,
Lady Brute, Lady Lurewell, Biddy Tipkin, Indiana.

Her two new plays were *The Humours of Oxford* by the
Reverend James Miller of Wadham College, which lasted a
week, and James Thomson's first play *Sophonisba*, which ran
twelve nights. Besides, she spoke the epilogue on the first night
of Benjamin Martyn's *Timoleon*, a play which ' burnt with
liberty and love '. For the last time the raffish audience clapped
the *double entendres* that fell from the lips of the dying actress:

> Well, sirs, whoe'er may take our Author's part,
> For me, I own I hate him at my heart.
> What? Shock the ladies with his odious rapes
> And draw the virtuous into filthy scrapes?
> To such vile licence now bold bards are grown
> That women scarce can call their own – their own!
> Well, poor Cleone had a ravenous lover,
> A piteous conflict – thank her stars 'tis over.
> Nay, frown not, ladies, make the case your own.
> What could she do? Eh? What would *you* have done?
> Not have consented sure. . . .?
> Yet when from friends removed, all ears at distance,
> A strong gallant, much love and no assistance,
> Who could have blamed the doctrine then of Non-resistance?

In *The Humours of Oxford* Anne played the part of the blue-
stocking, Lady Science. The Press reported that, whereas the
piece had been rehearsed with great applause before a small
audience, it was acted before a great audience with no applause
at all. One of its scenes, a donnish satire on the popular taste
for spectacle, with Pegasus, played by a donkey, emerging from
the summit of Mount Parnassus, sounds as if it might have
justified the ' ill-grounded cavils of the irrational and prejudiced
part of the town '.

Sophonisba is now only remembered for the line, ' Oh
Sophonisba! Sophonisba Oh! ' that Fielding parodied into:

> Oh! Huncamunca, Huncamunca Oh!
> Thy panting breasts like kettledrums of brass
> Beat everlasting loud alarms of joy.
> As bright as brass they are and oh! as hard;
> Oh! Huncamunca, Huncamunca Oh!

In its day the play created a prodigious amount of interest. New costumes and magnificent new sets were ordered. Every rehearsal was dignified (one wonders what the triumvirate was thinking about) with a splendid audience, even if the cynical remarked that no one was much affected. At the first rehearsal Thomson read his script, and he always read as if he did not understand his own lines. He was rather tall and fat with a dull, gross face. He was normally shy and silent, with nothing, said the beaux, of the gentleman in his person or his address. But Voltaire, who knew him well, ' liked in him the poet and the true philosopher. I think that without a good stock of such a philosophy, a poet is just above a fiddler who amuses our ears and cannot go to our soul.' *Sophonisba*, the Frenchman found, was well conceived and elegantly written, but it lacked fire. If the author could have been a little more interesting, he would have revivified English tragedy to which Shakespeare had given birth, and which, in Voltaire's opinion, he had then proceeded to ruin.

It was an anxious first night. When it was over, the poet joined his friends at a tavern on the Piazza with his wig as wet with sweat as if it had been dipped in an oil pot. But all was well. His poetry was allowed by the best judges to have been hardly inferior to any heard on the stage for many years. He was presented by the Earl of Grantham to the King and permitted to present a copy of the play.

His success he owed to Anne. She played the captive Queen of Carthage whose devotion to her country is the theme of the play. Carthage stood for England and Rome for France:

> . . . . Romans are the scourge
> Of the red world, destroyers of mankind;
> The ruffians, ravagers of earth – and all
> Beneath the smooth, dissimulating mask
> Of justice and compassion, as if ' slave '
> Were but another word for civilised. . . .
> . . . . While fair Carthage
> Unblemished rises on the base of commerce
> And asks of Heaven nought but the general winds
> And common tides that carry plenty, joy,
> Civility and grandeur round the world.

When Mrs Oldfield came to the lines:

> Meddle not with Carthage . . .
> . . . . not one base word of Carthage
> On thy soul. . . .

she spoke the words with such grandiose gesture, so tremulous a look and so penetrating a voice that she stopped the play. Praise was unanimous. Her performance was described as surprising; perhaps the critics had guessed her state of health. They testified that ' Mrs Oldfield has charmed all the world with the justice, force and gracefulness of her acting '. James Thomson himself wrote that she had excelled ' what even in the fondness of an author I could either wish or imagine. The grace, dignity and happy variety of her acting have been universally applauded as truly admirable.'

What playing this long and intensely difficult part cost her, few had any idea. Chetwood the prompter was to write with the wisdom of hindsight that the play was considered the cause of her death, ' for in her execution she went beyond wonder to astonishment. From that time her decay came slowly on.' In her suffering, her words as she received the poison cup, ' The first of blessings, Death ', must have had a categorical meaning for her. The poignancy of the lines that follow passed over the heads of her moist-eyed audience:

> Death appears not in a dreary light,
> Seems not a blank to me: a losing all
> Those fond sensations, those enchanting dreams
> Which cheat a toiling world from day to day. . . .

and so on down to her farewell to the England she loved so well:

> Oh never, never, Carthage
> Shall I behold thee more.

The poet Campbell did less than justice to a brother bard and a dying actress when he celebrated Anne's ' graceful features and spirited mien that could put life into tragedy – even Thomson's *Sophonisba* '.

Anne had always an instinct for detecting genius, for Savage's poem *The Wanderer* must be allowed something more than talent. Fielding and Thomson owed much to her. It was not her fault that of these three youthful protégés, not one had any real bent for the stage, the only field in which she could really help. Savage's two plays are not comparable to his poetry, Fielding's early successes on the stage have been quite forgotten in his fame as a novelist, while Thomson is now only read by the discerning for his *Seasons* and *Castle of Indolence*.

Less than a week of rest, if pain ever let her rest, and the bills were up for Anne's last benefit *The Fair Penitent* by Their Majesties' command. Is it fanciful to see significance in her choice of the character of a woman who has sinned and has repented? Altamonte was to be played by Wilks, Horatio by Mills, Lavinia by Mrs Horton and Calista by Mrs Oldfield. Lothario was to be acted by ' A Gentleman '. This was John Highmore of Hampton Court, who at White's had bet a nobleman of his acquaintance that he would play the part. The hit he made encouraged him to dip deeper into theatrical finance and before long he had bought the ailing Booth's interest in Drury Lane for three thousand pounds. Besides the play there was dancing by Mrs Booth, once the beautiful Miss Santlow. No one was admitted to the Boxes or behind the scenes except with a printed ticket which cost him five shillings. The Pit had been raised to three shillings and footmen were allowed to keep places on the stage for their mistresses. Even so, so great was the competition that ' several ladies of the first rank were excluded from want of room '.

Soon Anne had plunged into the benefit nights of her fellow artists. How could she refuse *The Spanish Friar* for Mrs Porter, *The Way of the World* for Mrs Booth, *The Provok'd Wife* for Mrs Thurmond with a part ' played by a young gentlewoman being her first attempt on any stage ' (the young gentlewoman was Cibber's unsatisfactory daughter Charlotte Charke)? The list goes on: *The Man of Mode* for Anne's rival Mrs Horton, *The Relapse* for Benjamin Johnson, *Jane Shore* for Tom Williams, *Love for Love* for Dicky Norris, *The Tender Husband* for Theophilus Cibber. . . .

On 28 April 1730 she played Lady Brute in Vanbrugh's *Provok'd Wife*. She was acting for the benefit of Miss Rafter, later known as Catherine Clive. She had always helped the young generation. This was the last time Anne Oldfield set foot on the stage.

CHAPTER XXV

After a well-graced actor leaves the stage. . . .

SHAKESPEARE

Curtain

AFTER THIS last performance Anne had six more months to live. They were months of pain, assuaged but little by the empiric skill of eighteenth-century physicians. Small doses of arsenic were the standard treatment with opium to soothe the agony. The doctors conducted an examination and diagnosed cancer, no doubt secondary, in the reproductive organs, a verdict which was confirmed later by a post-mortem. When they had finished their investigation, Anne earnestly begged them not to hide anything from her, but to give their opinion freely. They said gravely that they feared the disease was fatal. She showed no sign of shock or emotion and answered, accepting the lot God had assigned. She prayed that she might bear with patience what was to come.

She was not a religious woman in the conventional sense. Moving in the cynical, freethinking circles of Whig intellectual and aristocratic society in the Augustan age, it would have been hard for any outward show of faith to have survived. She was not, as has been supposed, the Narcissa of Pope's lines:

> Narcissa's nature tolerably mild,
> To make a wash would hardly stew a child. . . .
> A very heathen in the carnal part
> Yet still a sad good Christian at her heart.

That satire is levelled at the Duchess of Hamilton and confusion has arisen from Pope's use of the same pseudonym when quoting ' the last words that poor *Narcissa* spoke '. Anne's stoical submission to Divine Providence was none the less sincere.

On 27 June 1730 she sent for her lawyer and made her will. Her house, for which two thousand two hundred pounds had recently been paid, she left to her son Charles Churchill, as she no doubt promised her lover when he bought it for her. If

Charles died before he was twenty-one and left no children, the house was to go to her elder son, Arthur Maynwaring, or if he had died to her lover, Brigadier Churchill. The rest of her estate, except what was already invested in the funds or other public securities (and rumour credited her with five thousand pounds in South Sea Stock, then standing at over 103) was to be sold at once. This sale was not meant to include the trinkets she meant to give her friends. From the sum accruing, which was to be invested in government stocks chosen by her executors, she left a legacy of five thousand pounds to her son Arthur Maynwaring: four thousand pounds more than his father had been able to bequeath him. This was to be paid in the form of annual interest, until he should reach the age of thirty when he would inherit the capital. If he died, the money was to go to her son Charles, or if he did not survive Arthur, to his father the Brigadier. To her mother she left an immediate payment of ten guineas and an annual allowance of sixty pounds. To her aunt, Jane Gourlay, a similar immediate payment of ten guineas and an annuity of ten pounds which was to terminate on her mother's death. It may be presumed that the elder Mrs Oldfield was living with Jane. To her dresser she left an annuity of ten pounds for life. On the deaths of these three minor beneficiaries, such of her estate as was not disposed of was to be divided into three shares, two of which were to go to Arthur and one to Charles, or to the Brigadier if they had both died. As executors she appointed Lord Hervey, John Hedges of Finchley and Brigadier Churchill. According to the Press, she left each executor twenty pounds for mourning, if he would accept it, and twenty pounds to each of her servants.

One other business matter Anne was careful to settle. Her salary at Drury Lane had by now been raised to twelve guineas a week. In 1729 she was paid four hundred and twenty pounds salary, sixty pounds for her benefit and a bonus of forty guineas. Besides this the management allowed her one hundred pounds to buy her own dresses. Since Anne knew she would never act again, she notified the managers that she would accept no further payments on any count.

As summer came, her doctors, ' finding the disease baffled the force of their choicest medicines ', advised her to try country air. She chose Hampstead, mindful of the old days when Arthur was so ill. She did not stay there long. It is to be hoped that Grub Street was seeking sensation in writing that ' her pain did force such dismal shrieks from her that it was thought best to take her back '. At all events she soon returned to Grosvenor Street.

She lay on the damask bed, and waited hopefully for death. Churchill sat beside her. There was little he could do, but his presence soothed her. After a time the strain and grief were too much for him and he fell ill. Then she was alone with Margaret Saunders, who sat with her day and night. She could talk to her, when talking was possible, of the theatre and the autumn season that had begun without her. Mrs Horton was playing her part of Marcia in *Cato*, the part she had played when she was carrying Arthur's child. If it had lived . . . She wondered what sort of a showing Mrs Horton could make. She was too weak to care.

Margaret listened for any wish how she was to be buried; but Anne gave no sign. Should a clergyman be sent for? Anne had lived without them and would die without them. Of the Christian virtues, sobbed the dresser, she certainly possessed fortitude; all who knew her would witness she had never done a base or ungenerous thing.

The dying woman now could hardly speak but, said Margaret, ' she expressed herself in broken words and pious meditations, in the most moving way you could imagine. It may be justly said, she prayed without ceasing ' – or did good Margaret take the mutterings of delirium for prayers?

Thursday, 22 October, Anne's last day on earth, came. In St James's Park an appreciative crowd watched a private in the Footguards receive two hundred lashes for blasphemy. The Court moved from Windsor to Richmond. It was the Princess Royal's birthday and Mr Rich, that master of spectacle, by royal command prepared a masque in Kew Gardens. Over one thousand lamps, ' disposed in a very elegant manner ', were lit and fireworks sent up from Kew Green. But Anne Oldfield, who had been the central figure in so many command performances, was indifferent. She was in a coma. In the early hours of Friday she died.

At Drury Lane that night the house was dark.

Anne, if the Press may be believed, had expressed a wish, if not in the hearing of Mrs Saunders, that her funeral should be held in private. But Brigadier-General Churchill and his imposing friends, Lord Hervey and Sir Robert Walpole, thought otherwise. So famous an actress and so prominent a figure in society rated a public funeral – a funeral indeed in the Abbey. Did anyone object that her life had not been exemplary, that unworthy criticism could be countered by mention of her impeccable principles. So good a Whig should be buried anywhere the Whigs pleased!

So on Saturday a delegation attended the Dean and Chapter of Westminster to arrange for an Abbey burial. Mrs Saunders dressed her mistress for the last time ' in the nicety of dress that had been her delight when living '. On Tuesday the be-laced body was carried from Grosvenor Street to the Jerusalem Chamber, where it lay in state. About eleven at night, it was taken to the Abbey, supported by John, Baron de la Warr, Lieutenant-Colonel in the Guards, John, Baron Hervey of Ickworth, Privy Councillor and Vice-Chamberlain, the Right Honourable George Bubb Doddington, Lord of the Treasury, Charles Hedges, Walter Carey and Captain Elliot. Arthur Maynwaring junior was chief mourner and the Reverend Doctor Barker, Senior Prebendary, read the service.

Certain censorious persons tried to produce ' an obsolete Popish canon ' which prohibited the burial of actors in churches. The Prebendary showed greater breadth of mind and even a sense of humour when he replied that he had buried Mrs Oldfield very willingly and with the greatest satisfaction. A section of the Press which had been always hostile, expressed the hope that on the monument which would doubtless be erected, mention would be made of her Christian as well as her *moral* virtues. The same point of view was taken later by the Reverend Joseph Wilcox, the Dean of Westminster succeeding Samuel Bradford, who had consented to the actress's burial. When in February 1736 Brigadier Churchill applied for leave to put up a monument in the Abbey and an inscription to Anne's memory, the new Dean replied that he was so far from thinking the matter proper to be granted that he could neither consent to it himself, nor put any question of it to the Chapter. So Anne was left uncommemorated but for a stone with her name and the date of her death near the west end of the South Aisle, appropriately close to the monument of Congreve, for whom her lover had acted as pall-bearer some eighteen months before.

Conversation between a statesman, a poet, a physician, a bishop and an actress as they lay buried together in the Abbey was subsequently published. The first was James Craggs the younger, the poet Congreve, the doctor John Freind and the bishop Atterbury.

Atterbury (to Anne)	Well, if we must bear with your company, pray be a little further.
Anne	Lie a little further, sir? 'Tis the first time I am ever treated so rudely.
Atterbury	Why did not you enquire first if we were fit for your tune?
Anne	Because I used to be welcome anywhere. And had you any life amongst you all, you had gone together by the ears for the next place to my coffin.
Congreve	Oh! madam, times are altered now. Our gallantry and your beauty die together.
Anne	Times are altered indeed when poets give themselves such airs. Don't I remember twenty of you together sneaking for a look or a smile?

What, one wonders, would be the comments of a twentieth-century intruder on this corner of the Abbey, Chief Scout of All the World, Lord Baden-Powell?

Plenty of epitaphs were published. Many mourned her sincerely:

> Grateful to Oldfield's sweet, much-honoured shade
> For matchless pleasure. . . .

Richard Savage wore black for her; he also deplored the lost allowance. The Drury Lane prompter evinced a note of genuine, if flowery, emotion:

The sun rises to set again, but Oldfield's light is lost for ever. I was too young to view her first dawn on the stage. But yet the infinite satisfaction of her meridian lustre, a glow of charms not to be beheld but with a trembling eye!

The Gentleman's Magazine in its first year printed the Latin epitaph that it considered should have been cut to Anne's memory. In English it reads:

> Near this place among so many celebrated poets
> Rests the body of
> ANNE OLDFIELD
> Herself not less deserving to be celebrated,
> For whenever she trod the stage,
> Her acting always illustrated
> And ennobled
> Their compositions.
> Never was one genius so well adapted to
> The most different poets.
> She seemed born for each distinctly.
> In Tragedy
> Her noble presence, elevated speech and
> Majestic gait, tempered with so peculiar
> Sweetness of voice,
> Never failed to transport the
> Most rustic and insensitive with admiration.
> In Comedy
> She discovered such a winning air, such a
> Sprightly and becoming gaiety
> And so delicate an address,
> That neither eyes were satisfied with seeing
> Nor hands weary of applauding.

Thus justly was commemorated Anne's genius on the stage. Her courage, gaiety, generosity, wisdom and wit were left unregarded.

Index